FOREWORD

I BELIEVE if a person is willing to read what we have in this book, observe and analyze the work of other horseshoers, and practice what is discussed here, then that person will be able to learn to shoe most horses. In this book we stress good horse handling techniques and proper trimming. Correct trimming of the feet is the basis of good shoeing, and neither can be accomplished if the horseshoer cannot get the horse to stand still long enough to work on him—thus the importance of handling.

A person can use this book as a guide, to learn whether his horse is being shod properly, or he can use it to learn to shoe his own horse, if that is the goal. But to get really proficient at horseshoeing it takes a lot of practice trimming and shoeing a lot of different horses. For anyone who wants to use this book as a start to becoming a farrier who shoes for the public, I suggest you spend about $200 for hand tools and practice with them for 6 to 8 weeks. That should be enough time to figure out whether you are physically able to do the work. After that, if you are willing to proceed, you can invest some more money in equipment.

The ideal situation for a person just starting out to become a farrier is to find someone with a bunch of horses who is willing to let you trim their feet for no pay. There are still a lot of places that will let a beginner do this as long as he treats their horses well. Later on, if you have a chance to ride along with a veteran horseshoer, you should take advantage of that, because you need to round out your education, and this added experience will help develop your eye. Your eye is a real important factor in shoeing—if a person cannot observe and analyze a horse's way of going, cannot get the proper depth perception and figure the angle for trimming a foot, then it will be hard to learn how to do these things well. A lot of people attend horseshoeing schools, and receive good educations in the process. But in my opinion, a student still needs to work on many more horses over time to be completely proficient as a shoer.

The main difference in horseshoeing today, compared to what it was like in the past, is that the horseshoer generally goes to the horses. Years ago, the horses were taken to the shoer in the blacksmith shop. There is another difference, too, in that today we have a wide range of manufactured shoes and related materials that work very well for the horseshoer. We no longer have to make most of our own horseshoes on the forge.

—*Don Baskins*

CONTENTS

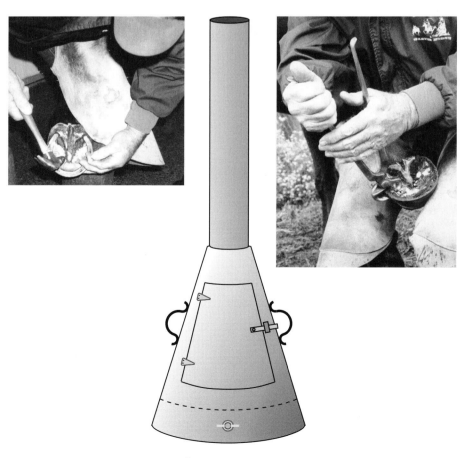

A *WESTERN HORSEMAN* BOOK

Well-Shod

A Horseshoeing Guide for Owners & Farriers

By Don Baskins
With Randy Witte

Illustrations by Dwayne Brech

Photographs by Fran Devereux Smith, Kathy Swan,
Rick Swan, Gary Vorhes, Randy Witte

Well-Shod

Published by
WESTERN HORSEMAN® magazine

3850 North Nevada Ave.
Box 7980
Colorado Springs, CO 80933-7980

www.westernhorseman.com

Design, Typography and Production
Western Horseman
Colorado Springs, Colorado

Cover photograph by
Kathy Swan

Printing
Branch Smith
Fort Worth, Texas

©1997 by Western Horseman
a registered trademark of
Morris Communications Corporation
725 Broad Street
Augusta, GA 30901
All rights reserved
Manufactured in the United States of America

Tenth Printing: November 2005

ISBN 0-911647-69-4

DEDICATION

To my beautiful
wife and helpmate, Oda.

Don Baskins

DON BASKINS

MEET DON BASKINS

Don and one of his clients.

THE FIRST TIME Don Baskins came to our Tesquesquite Ranch was in 1964, after he had met my father, Albert J. Mitchell, at a sorority function their wives were attending. My father asked Don to come to our ranch and shoe a few horses the following week. When Don arrived to do the shoeing, he was taken to a corral of 20 unshod ranch horses. That afternoon, when Don had finished shoeing the horses, he went up to my grandfather's house to be paid.

Grandfather was the late Albert K. Mitchell, a tall, honest man in the horse and cattle business. He was a founding member of the American Quarter Horse Association, and he was also a cowboy who knew how difficult some of the ranch horses could be to shoe. Don told him the 20 horses had been shod, and Grandfather must have eyed him suspiciously.

"Nobody can shoe 20 of my horses in one day," he said. And he went down to the corral to look for himself. Much to his surprise, all the horses were standing around with newly shod hoofs. He returned to the house and paid Don for the work, and never again did Albert K.

Mitchell question Don's word or ability.

Since that day, Don became a constant visitor to our ranch. The Tequesquite Ranch continues to raise high-quality Quarter Horses, and Don is the man who keeps them trimmed and shod. I remember, as a child, watching him work on 15 or 20 horses in the corral, trimming and shoeing one right after the other. Then he would come to the house to visit with Mother and hold me on his lap. The big strong horseshoer has always had a soft spot in his heart for little girls, and today my nieces are happy to see him, and they are the ones who crawl up into his big arms.

The driving force behind Don is his family: his wife, Oda, who he says is the most beautiful woman he ever met, and three grown children—John Bradley, Cara Dawn, and Sarah Beth.

Don drives a five-state area, making his horseshoeing rounds. He has shod champion reiners, cutters, barrel horses, pleasure horses, rope horses, and race horses. He has also worked on bulls, mules, donkeys, and draft horses. Even though he works for a lot of top people in the horse industry, he always has time to stop by Mosquero, N.M., and shoe one horse for his old cowboy friend, Tony Griego, or to trim or shoe 4-H horses for the youngsters on his list.

Don is the only horseshoer I know who has worked for the same family for three generations. He is loyal to his customers, whether they are famous trainers or folks who simply have an old pet horse in their backyards. He also has a world of knowledge and likes to teach people who are willing to listen and learn. His book has a lot to offer to aspiring horseshoers and to persons who simply want to learn about horseshoeing and know whether their horses are being shod properly.

—*Lynda M. Ray*

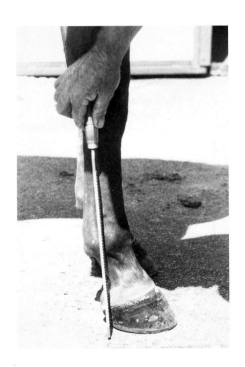
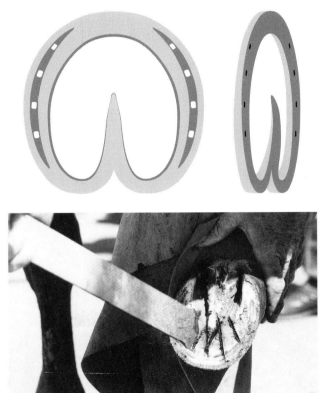
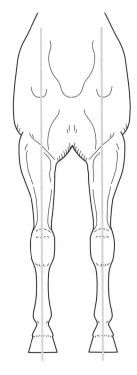

RECOLLECTIONS OF REMUDAS AND BIG RANCHES

Those ranch horses were just not broke well enough to where a guy could rely on them not kicking while being saddled.

MOST OF THE business I got when I first arrived in New Mexico was on big ranches. These ranches had never had a horseshoer. They had big strings of saddle horses, maybe 100 to 400 head of saddle horses, and one reason they carried those big remudas was because there was no one to shoe them.

The horses were ridden barefoot, most of the time, and they were rotated. A horse might be ridden part of a day, perhaps gathering cattle in rough country, then turned back into the herd for a week or more because he was sore-footed and needed time to recover.

Any horses who were shod were shod by the cowboys, who had to take time away from their regular chores and spend an inordinate amount of time shoeing horses who, more than likely, were not used to being handled a lot, and were not very cooperative.

But spending money to have their horses shod proved to be a good investment for those ranches. The owners found that it was cost effective. A cowboy no longer had to spend part of a day, or maybe part of a couple days, shoeing a horse who fought his efforts. The cowboys could be doing other work around the ranch, instead. The owners also found they no longer needed to maintain such large remudas when gathering and working cattle. And another benefit was that the horses became a lot gentler because of the extra handling they received while being shod on a regular basis.

A lot of the cowboys, when saddling those horses, would wisely use the latigo to reach under the horses' bellies to snare their cinches, rather than reach under by hand and risk getting kicked. Those ranch horses were just not broke well enough to where a guy could rely on them not kicking while being saddled. But, over the next 2 or 3 years of regular handling, it was obvious that the number of horse-related accidents to cowboys had declined. The horses were getting gentler to handle, and because their feet were kept trimmed and shod they were not as likely to stumble and fall while being ridden.

I remember the first time I went to Albert K. Mitchell's Lazy K Ranch, at Albert, New Mexico. The ranch carried about 300 saddle horses at the time. I had talked with Albert Mitchell about shoeing his horses, and made an appointment to do some of them. I'll never forget that day.

A couple of hands roped out 21 head of horses and put them in a pen, and then turned the rest of the horses out. They asked if I needed any help, and I told them no, that I worked by myself, and got along better with most horses just tied up or ground-tied or whatever was feasible. The cowboys had caught about two horses for each of the bosses and the owner, and the rest of the twenty-one head consisted of a horse out of each cowboy's string.

I started catching those horses and working on them, and guessed that they were used to people fighting them to get some shoes nailed on for perhaps hours at a time. I think I worked too fast for a lot of those horses' minds, because I finished shoeing all 21 head by about 4 in the afternoon. I went up to the big house to get paid, and told Albert K. that I had done 21 head of horses, and was charging $7 a

The late Albert K. Mitchell of the Lazy K Ranch (also known as the Tequesquite Ranch), Albert, N.M., is pictured horseback in the 1960s on the only stocking-legged horse he ever cared to ride—a gelding named Socks. This horse was first shod when he was about 10 years old, and I was the farrier who did the work. Mr. Mitchell, who served 4 years as president of the American Quarter Horse Association, preferred solid sorrel horses as a rule, but he thought a lot of Socks. Albert K. was a gentleman and a cowboy. Check his necktie.

Photo by Morton

They decided that 10 shod horses were better than 100 unshod horses. In two or three shoeings, all those horses got to be good to work on.

horse. He just looked at me.

"There is no man alive who can shoe 21 head of my horses in a day," he said.

"Well, Mr. Mitchell," I said, "they are all there in the corral."

So he went outside and got on a little Cushman motor scooter, and rode from the big house down to the horse corral to inspect the horses. I stayed behind and waited for him, and in a little while he came back, went inside the house, and wrote a check for me. I've been doing horses on that ranch ever since.

The Lazy K used to take 100 head of horses up on the north end of the big ranch to work cattle there. It took them 2 or 3 weeks, generally, to go up there and brand that end of the ranch—it had something like 90 to 100 sections. I don't remember how many cows they ran up there, but with all those horses they used for the work, it seemed like they spent half their time hunting horses and penning them, changing horses, and hunting more horses.

I talked to Mr. Mitchell about shoeing 10 horses for him—1 for each man going up there to work. I suggested he take those shod horses in the trailer, and not have to spend a day or two trailing a big remuda to the area. He could keep those 10 head penned, and just work out of the pens each day, gathering cows and calves, branding. Sure enough, that's what they did that year, and they got all the work done in about 6 days. They decided that 10 shod horses were a lot better than 100 unshod horses.

In two or three shoeings, all those horses got to be good to work on. The horses I still shoe there are well-broke and are probably the best horses to shoe in the whole state of New Mexico.

Another big ranch I did a lot of work for was the Moon Ranch at Buckhorn, New Mexico. It was owned by Mr. and Mrs. Leroy Spiers at the time, and they had a remuda of about 400 head of saddle horses. A lot of those horses were used for packing salt to cattle. That is malpais (lava rock) country, and horseshoes lasted only

a ride or two, and then the horse had to be shod again.

When the ranch cowboys were getting ready for branding, they would start by shoeing all those horses; then they would use horses one after another gathering cattle in that rough country. Those malpais rocks really grind off horseshoes in short order.

The ranch left the bulls in with the cows year-round, and they branded calves twice a year and shipped twice a year, so the outfit really did need a lot of horses under those conditions. But they found that by having a horseshoer come and stay while they were working they could get by with a lot fewer horses, and maybe shoe those horses three or four times each during the works. I used to ride and help them some when I was there shoeing, and found if you went to the top of one of those big malpais hills and rode enough to gather some cattle off the side hills and put them down into the trails that had been made with bulldozers, you could grind off a set of shoes in one or two rides.

When I used to do horses at the Moon Ranch, I would get up early and have a couple of the hands catch horses. Each man would then help by holding two horses in the barn aisle. In other words, there were four horses lined up in the barn—four abreast—throughout most of the day. I would start down between those horses, trimming a front foot on this horse, a front foot on the next, and doing the same with the back feet. Then I would work back through them, trimming the other feet, go to the anvil to fit the shoes, then throw four shoes under each horse. All I had to do then was pick up shoes off the floor, one by one, and nail them on.

Those horses would stand good for this type of operation, mainly because they were comfortable standing together. If I separated those horses, and tried to do them one at a time, I was generally in trouble. A lot of times I would shoe from 16 to 20 head like this in just a matter of 6 to 8 hours. Then I would take off and rest for 2 or 3 hours and maybe do another bunch of horses. This was an easy way to work, for me. I didn't waste much time

Fall branding crew on the Tequesquite Ranch in New Mexico, early 1970s. Lots of good Hereford cattle, and lots of country. The ranch still brands several times a year, and still raises and rides good Quarter Horses.

going back and forth to the anvil, and feet were always right by me.

When I was shoeing out at the works, we would tie horses next to one another, four together, to a wagon or tree, and I would shoe them in a bunch like that and get along fine. They were used to being shod together.

The first time I went to the Moon Ranch, we started shoeing horses early, getting ready to go to the works. About 2 o'clock in the afternoon, Mr. Spiers came to the barn and saw that I was nearly done shoeing the bunch of horses they had gathered that morning.

He suggested to his grandson, whom he called "Charlie Boy," that he go gather some more horses for me. Charlie Boy said, "Don't you think the man gets tired?

He is going just as fast now as when he started."

A lot of times I shod as many as 40 horses a day there, and that's a pretty big run for most shoers. To do it, a person must get himself prepared mentally, and get his business straight, to know exactly what he is going to do and be able to fit shoes without going back and forth to the anvil a lot. A person can learn to do herds of horses like that, and fix them to where you can get the best service out of them. Of course, shoeing horses for use in those

Broodmares and foals on the Mitchells' Tequesquite Ranch, Albert, New Mexico.

Photos by Harvey Caplin

malpais rocks, I didn't have to finish their feet up like I do for show horses. I would drive the nails and turn them over, and move on to the next one.

Another ranch I worked was Frank Parks' place at Hooker, Oklahoma. Mr. Parks kept between 600 and 700 head of horses in corrals, pens, and runs. All those horses were in pens by age and sex, with eight to ten to fifteen horses in each enclosure. They were all pets, to him, and most had never been halter-broke. But that old man could go in and pet them and talk to them, sometimes put a halter on and drop the rope, and those horses would stand for me to trim their feet. Still, I had to learn to kind of creep around those horses, and it was one

of the biggest jobs I ever undertook.

Whenever Mr. Parks decided to have the work done, he would call my wife and say, "Honey, if you can get that boy over here, I'll send you a nice present." As soon as I would get there, the old man would slip off and send her a $100 bill. That's the way he kept me coming back.

Finally, I got the horses broke down to where I did them in different sections. I would go and trim so many yearlings one time, so many 2-year-olds the next, and leave about a half-day open to where I could go through and catch anything that had gotten in a bad way. Most of those horses were trimmed about four times a year, and their feet stayed in reasonably good condition for not being used.

When I started doing those horses, I was getting $2 a horse to trim. I got to where I could go through there and trim anywhere from 50 to 75 horses a day,

12

which was pretty good, considering those horses were basically not broke. The first time I went to Mr. Parks' place, the old gentleman wrote a check for me, and I could hardly read the check because his writing was so bad.

I said, "Mr. Parks, how am I going to cash this check? I can hardly read it."

He replied, "You go down there to my bank. There's fellers in there who can read."

I did Mr. Parks' work for about 10 years. Before he passed away, I never paid for a meal or room in Hooker. He had always been there ahead of me and arranged to pay for everything. That was a pretty good relationship with that old fellow. Most of the guys that had tried to work for him as horse trainers had been fired at gun-point. No one came on his place and spurred one of his horses or roughed up one in any way.

Years ago, when a lot of those outfits had production sales, I would go ahead of time and trim feet on all the horses, pull their manes and tails, and use clippers on them to really clean them up for the sale. I did well at this, because most of the people who were raising a lot of horses didn't have enough help to get them ready for a

public auction. It was a good deal for me because I could get along with the horses since I had taken care of their feet.

There are not nearly as many ranch production sales as there used to be, but it is still good, necessary work for a young shoer when he can find it. For most of the horses around a ranch like that, the horse-shoer is the only one who has handled them a good share of the time. As a rule, you can get a deal worked out to go help put on the sale, cleaning up the horses, and getting them through the sale ring.

Getting to know the different families of horses has always been interesting and helpful to me. It is to the point where, if I have a new horse to shoe, and I know how he is bred, I can pretty well predict what his feet will be like to work on, how he will react to being caught and shod, and some of his idiosyncrasies. It helps to know the characteristics of the different families of horses.

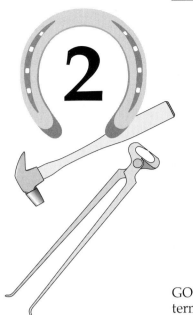

HORSE HANDLING TIPS

By working with the horse until he thinks I am probably all right, I will have less trouble shoeing him.

GOOD HORSEMANSHIP—as the term applies to handling, managing, and understanding horses—is important to a horseshoer. Approaching the horse, catching him, and working on the horse are essential to getting him trimmed and shod.

I prefer to catch a horse myself, especially a horse who is new to me. This gives me a chance to analyze the horse and see what he's like. If the horse is hard to catch, he will probably be hard to approach when I put on my apron and carry my box to him.

Introducing myself to a new horse is important. If the owner leads such a horse to me, I like to take the halter rope and hold it myself. That way I can look him in the eye, rub him over the eye with my hand, and let him get acquainted with me before I start shoeing. By working with the horse until he thinks I am probably all right, I will have less trouble shoeing him. It stands to reason that the softer, the easier, and gentler I can be around the horse, the easier he is going to be to shoe.

The look in a horse's eye, incidentally, can reveal a lot about the horse's disposition and how he will likely be to shoe. A big soft eye is generally an indication of a gentle nature. A small eye, especially a

1/ This horse walked away from me when I entered his pen. I let him settle and he went to a corner.

2/ When he stopped and looked at me, I approached, then touched his face.

small eye with "white side-walls" around it, as a general rule is an indication that the horse will have some bad thoughts about being shod. This difference in eyes may have something to do with vision, with how well a horse can see around himself, which in turn may influence his disposition. There are exceptions to the rule, but when I approach a horse and see a "bad eye," I am alerted that this horse is probably not of the best disposition.

I never approach a horse with my hand out. Most horses have been made to move by someone hollering at them or sticking a hand out and waving it, so I know if I approach a horse in a pen and stick out my hand, then he is probably going to move away. A loose horse in a pen quite often will want to run around the pen when a stranger approaches, so I'll let a horse like that run to a corner, and then kind of "semi-corner" him. I will not put a lot of pressure on the horse, trying to actually corner him, but I will be in his quarter of the pen, and I just stand there, holding the halter. Nine times out of ten, that horse will then approach me. When he does, it is easy to reach up and rub his neck, and

3/ I moved my hand around to his neck . . .

4/ . . . reached up with the halter . . .

5/ . . . and proceeded to halter him.

bring the halter to his face and halter him. I call that "letting the horse catch you."

The same principle works in a stall or a large pasture (many times). In a stall, you just step inside the door and stand there a few seconds and, as a rule, the horse will turn and come to you. That's how I catch a lot of horses. By using this simple, quiet procedure, I can catch horses easier than some of their owners.

Of course, the feed bucket works well for catching a lot of horses too.

Another advantage to catching a horse myself—it gives me a chance to see how he moves and to analyze his feet.

I generally do not even put on my apron until after I have tested a new horse, to see whether he will let me pick up his front feet, and then his back feet. If a horse will let you pick up his feet, **he will probably be pretty easy to work on.**

To pick up a front foot on a new horse, I start by facing him, **then move to his shoulder, still facing the rear, then put my shoulder into his shoulder and my hand on his leg. I can then move my hand down** and press a finger somewhere below the knee on the side of the cannon bone. This causes the horse to relax his knee so I can lift up his foot.

To pick up a back foot on a strange horse, I put my hand on his hip, while facing to the rear, and move him off-center slightly by pushing on the hip. Then I move my outside hand down his leg.

Most horses who have a problem with shoeing have had a bad experience with a horseshoer. Or maybe the owners have inadvertently caused the problem. Whatever the reason, when I run across such a horse, my first objective is to work around him in a quiet, easy manner—not to fight him—and do what I can to gain his confidence, and show him I will not hurt him. I may take the horse back to his stall, or wherever he lives, and tie him up, then pick up his feet, pet him, and get him so he has no fear of me. Learning to take the time to do this is a big factor for success in shoeing horses.

After a horse gets accustomed to me, I can move more quickly and get more things done with him. It is important for the horseshoer to not lose his temper, especially while working on a horse like this, because the horse is scared, initially. If a person is rough in handling most horses, there is a good possibility he will not get along with them for shoeing or anything else.

Sometimes I can pare down a horse's foot and trim him, and get along fine, but when I nail on the shoe, he wants to pull his foot away. He is afraid of the hammer. Maybe someone hurt him with a nail last time, or cuffed him with the hammer and caused him to be bad about this part of the shoeing. Anyway, I have found if I start the nail and then alternately tap the shoe, I will usually regain the horse's confidence that the hammer will not hurt him.

I hit the nail, then tap the shoe, hit the nail, tap the shoe. And pretty soon the nail is driven. I drive an inside nail first, then an outside nail. If he is still "quivery" after a couple of nails have been placed, and **wants to pull his** foot away, I put that foot **down and go to another one.** Sometimes he will be better about nailing the other foot. Then when I go back to the original foot to finish it, quite often he will be fine about that foot too.

Very few horses need to be twitched or have a lip chain on them for shoeing. If most of them are just handled quietly, they will submit to shoeing if given a little time. If a horse is bad about leaning on you, while working on a back foot, it is probably because the stifle muscle has not yet relaxed. If you have allowed the stifle to relax and the horse is still bad about not wanting you to pick up a back foot, a horseshoer can reach up from beside the horse and take hold of his tail, near the base, then twist the tail counterclockwise. As soon as there is some stress on his tail, the horse will shift his weight off that foot and allow it to be picked up.

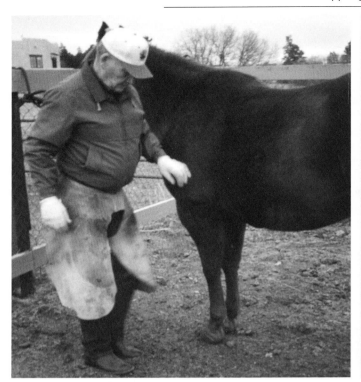

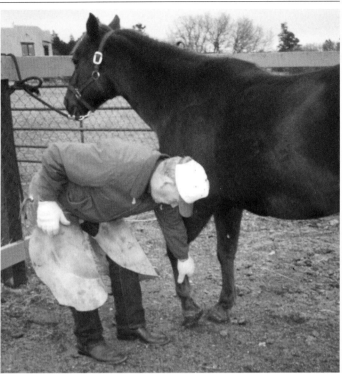

1/ Here is a standard method of picking up a front foot to clean it out with a hoof pick or to trim and shoe a horse. Start at his shoulder, facing to the rear.

2/ Run your hand down his leg, to the back of the cannon bone. Grasping this area with thumb and fingers will cause the horse to lift the foot.

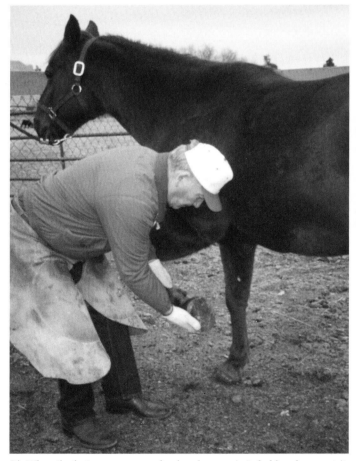

3/ When the foot comes up, my free hand moves in to hold and support it.

4/ From this position, I can then take a step toward the hindquarters . . .

5/ . . . and bring the foot between my legs, just above the knees, which holds the foot in place, thus freeing my hands to do what work needs to be done on the hoof.

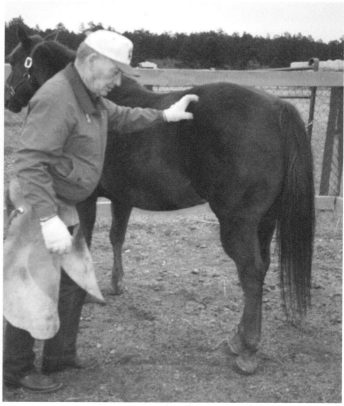

6/ To pick up a back foot, I start with my hand on the horse's hip . . .

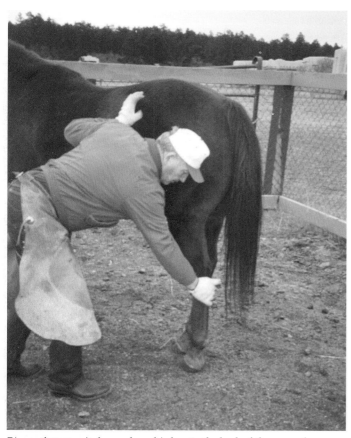

7/ . . . then run it down along his leg, to the back of the canon bone.

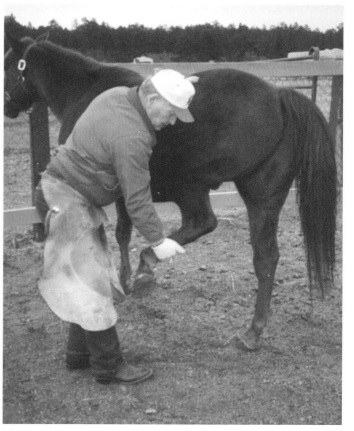

8/ This causes the horse to lift that foot.

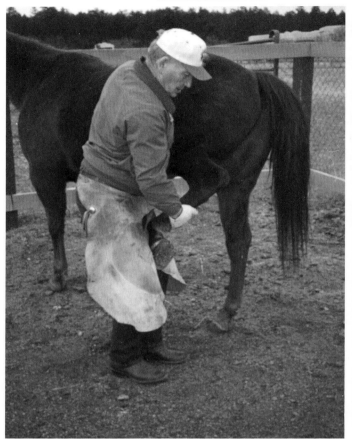

9/ The back leg is then cradled in my lap.

10/ The fetlock rests just above my knees.

When working on a foot, bend from the waist down— in your knees. Try to work at the end of your arms. You and the horse will both be more comfortable.

11/ Both my hands are now free to begin work on the hoof.

Holding the Horse

There is a correct way for a person to hold a horse being worked on by a horse-shoer, veterinarian, or anyone else. That person should stay on the same side of the horse as the person doing the work.

It is better if the holder will give the horse some slack—about a foot of shank. Then if the horse moves, take hold of the shank. It also helps if the horse is wearing a regular leather or nylon halter. He can feel a halter like that much better than he can feel a soft rope halter. The leather or heavy nylon halter will move when the lead shank is moved, and the horse will respond to it.

Holding the horse too tightly makes him think he is in a vise and might cause him to panic. You cannot physically force a horse to stand still. He must be trained to do so.

If the horse moves around, the holder can reach up and tug the mane or pet the horse with his other hand. Quite often this will settle the horse so the shoer can work on him. It does make the work a lot easier if the horse is not moving around and rubbing and pushing and shoving on the horseshoer.

I do not mind a horse reaching around and smelling or rubbing his nose on me when I have a front foot picked up. The horse is sensing that I am all right if he rubs on me a little like that, and very few horses will bite the horseshoer when he is bent over working. A lot of owners, holding a horse who does that, worry about it and then fuss with the horse, but the horse is just getting used to me, and it is a pretty good idea to let him do it.

Most horses are best to shoe if they are just tied up. I shoe a lot of horses in a cross-tie. Most horses stand well when cross-tied because that's where they are groomed and handled a lot. But if there is not a good cross-tie, or the horse has never been in a cross-tie before, I recommend tying him about 12 to 18 inches long to a flat wall, if possible, and tying his head up a little higher than normal.

The Short Rope Act

Sooner or later, a horseshoer will be confronted with trimming or shoeing a horse, young or old, who has not been trained sufficiently when it comes to having his feet handled. It could be a horse who is simply frightened over the prospect of a person trying to reach down and take away one of his feet, or a horse, maybe from past experience, who simply harbors some bad thoughts toward horse-shoers and what they want to do. Every successful horseshoer has had to learn to work on horses who are less than coopera-tive about their feet.

Through the ages, horses have been restrained for shoeing when necessary. The old-time blacksmith shops were well-equipped for this. They had devices to tie down or tie up every foot on a horse in order to get him trimmed and shod without risk of hurting the horse or the guy who was working on him. Simi-lar methods of restraint—the scotch hobble, for instance—have been employed successfully in the field.

A few years ago, however, I learned a procedure by accident that I have since refined to the point where I no longer have any use for any of the other methods of restraint. I call it The Short Rope Act (*Western Horseman*, May 1994). With this procedure, I can take away a horse's flight-or-fight instinct by using the loop end of a stiff nylon lariat that has been cut in half. The rapid transformation that comes over a horse, young or old, who does not want his feet picked up or worked with, is pretty amazing.

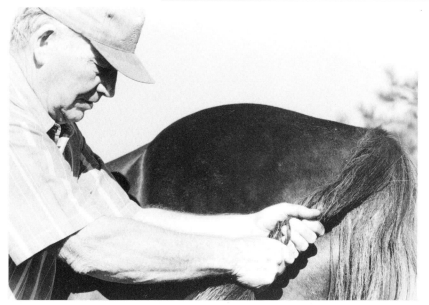

1/ If a horse is bad about not letting you pick up a hind foot, this little trick should solve the problem. Take his tail in hand, and slowly twist it counterclockwise.

3/ Keeping hold of the tail with one hand, I can move my other hand down his leg . . .

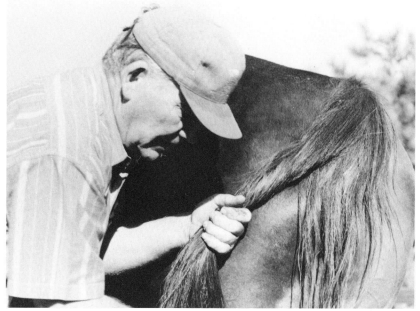

2/ As soon as there is some stress on the tail, the horse will shift his weight off that foot.

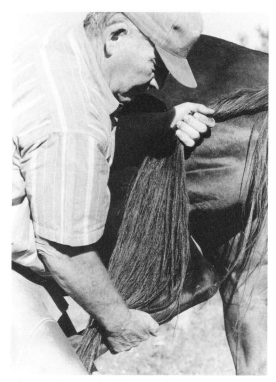

4/ . . . and proceed to lift up his foot.

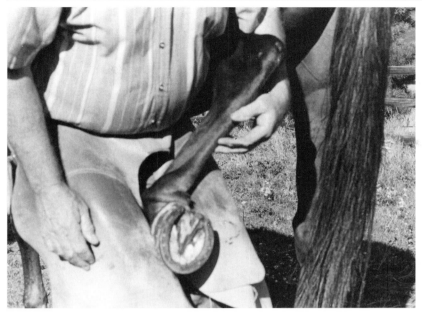

5/ *The hind foot moves to my lap, and I am ready to work on it.*

6/ *The tail twist can also be used to pick up a front foot. If a horse is applying weight to the foot I want to pick up, and refuses to let me have it, I can twist the tail as before and move to the front leg.*

7/ *When I see and feel his weight shift away from me, I can run my hand down the leg and pick it up.*

8/ *At this point, I am ready to release the tail.*

If a person is holding the horse while the farrier is working on him, it is best for the handler to stay on the same side the farrier is on, and to have about a foot of lead rope between the hand and the halter.

If a horse is to be tied up while the farrier works on him, try to always tie safely—at about eye level, if possible, and with a quick-release knot. Note that there is about a foot of lead rope between halter and knot. Tying next to a chainlink fence is not particularly desirable. A horse who pawed or kicked could possibly catch a foot in it. And tying to a corral pole or board is not safe. A horse who pulled back might pull the pole or board loose and then panic. This horse is actually tied to a stout post, however, and he is gentle and not apt to have a problem that would get him into the chainlink fence. He stood quietly to have his feet trimmed.

Here is a procedure for trimming mares and their foals (for the first time) that works well on one of the ranches I go to regularly. The mares and foals are corralled together— each mare is haltered and tied to the side of a pipe corral, while the foals mingle freely inside the corral. One at a time, a mare is then led out of the corral and into the covered end of the barn.

One word of caution: This method is not recommended for someone who lacks adequate experience with handling foals, horses, and ropes, and who does not have the proper pen to work in. For those who do have the necessary experience and facilities, this method can be safe for horse and handler alike. It works on foals who have not been handled a lot, and need their feet trimmed to keep their legs growing straight. It also works on older horses bad about having their feet worked on. The only difference between the two is that I like to have the older horses haltered and tied securely, rather than have them loose in a small pen, as I do the foals.

Here is an example of The Short Rope Act employed when I go to one ranch to trim broodmares and their foals for the first time.

The mares and foals are gathered from the pasture and corralled just outside a barn, where I do all the trimming at one end of a large alleyway. I trim a mare while her foal is loose, watching and wandering around nearby. Once the mare is trimmed, she is taken out a side door, with the youngster following behind. She is led through a small pipe pen (about 10 by 12 feet) just outside the door, and then taken through a gate, which is closed before the foal can pass through. The mare is tied outside the small pen, close to her baby, who by this time is showing some anxiety over the situation.

These foals have been handled minimally since birth, and are accustomed to running free in the pasture. The sight of me entering the pen with a short rope in my hand quickly sends a foal to the far corner.

I start by approaching the foal in a slow, nonthreatening manner, my body turned slightly sideways, avoiding direct eye contact. I build a small loop in the rope and hang it to my side. I then get as close as I can to the youngster and toss the loop on the ground, near one of his front feet. As soon as the foal steps into the loop (and this may take a couple of attempts before he does), I pull up the slack, catching the leg just above or below the knee.

Typically, this will send the foal scrambling to the other side of the pen. I just hold the tail of the rope in my hand and follow behind, but do not pull on the rope. Each foal will react a little differently—

I can trim the mare while her foal waits nearby. When I am done trimming the mare, I then do the foal, using what I call The Short Rope Act, shown in the next series of photos.

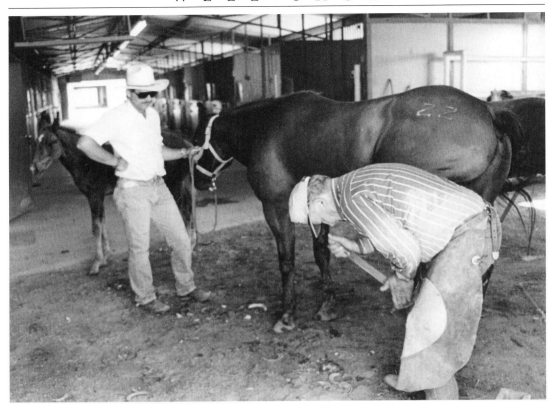

some run back and forth past me a time or two—but all eventually settle in a corner, facing away from me.

At this point, I gently maneuver the tail of the rope so it is rubbing around the hind legs. I get the foal to step over the rope so it is between the hind legs, and raise it up around each hock. The foal will subsequently turn one way or the other, perhaps move to the other side of the pen, but will soon stop in a corner, partially tangled in a loose rope. At no time do I try to restrain the foal with the rope. I just help him get a little tangled up with it around his legs, to the point where the foal obviously feels he is unable to flee.

With the youngster standing still at this point—and not looking particularly uncomfortable—I move up slowly till I am right next to him. Then I bend the tail of the rope into the shape of a horseshoe, and gently rub it around the foal's face, across his nose, above his eyes, and finally lift it

behind the ears and rub there too.

With the foal still standing quietly, one of the ranch hands enters the pen with a foal halter in hand, and with the hoof nippers and rasp in his pockets. The two of us will slip on the halter for the first time in that foal's life, and the foal accepts it and continues to stand quietly.

The assistant holds the halter rope while I lift up the front foot with the rope on it. I trim and rasp the hoof with no resistance from the foal. Then, working on the same side, I move to the back leg. The rope will still be on the foal's front leg, but I take the tail of the rope and rub it around the hock a little bit. I pick up the hind foot with the tail of the rope looped below the fetlock, then gently put the foot down.

At this point, the foal will be ready for me to pick up his back foot with my hand. To make sure the foal does not kick forward with the foot when I initially pick it up by hand, I first grasp the tail with one hand and slowly twist it counterclockwise. I then pick up the foot with my other hand, release the tail, and the assistant hands me the nippers.

Before trimming the other side, I take the tail of the rope and encircle the other

1/ I approached this youngster with a small loop built in my rope, prepared to catch either of the front legs (but not both) in the loop.

front leg, rubbing it back and forth around the knee, and then do the same around the hock of the back leg. The effect will be to give the foal that same sense of entanglement. Then I trim the front and back hoofs in the same manner as before. After that, the rope will be removed along with the halter, and the foal will walk off and be returned to his mother. The entire procedure, from the time I walk into the pen with the foal, will take maybe 15 minutes.

So far, The Short Rope Act has not failed me. And as I said, the procedure is the same for older horses, the only difference being that I like the older horses to be haltered and tied securely, from 12 to 18 inches, preferably to a solid wall. The older horses take more time than the babies, but they always come around. Everything else is the same. They may panic or fight the rope initially, but soon show signs of resignation, which is followed by relaxation, and finally, cooperation. I have not had to repeat the procedure on either a foal or mature horse when it was time to trim his feet again.

This little rope trick also helps prevent any horse from lying on you and pushing while you work on his feet. Some additional benefits: After the rope procedure has been used on horses who have been

2/ The foal moved back and forth from one side of the pen to the other a couple of times, then settled down. Note that the rope is attached just above the knee of the right leg. This is preferable to below the knee, and if I catch one below the knee, I will move it up by hand, first chance I get. Notice also at this point that I am beginning to get the youngster tangled up, with the rope running between the hind legs.

4/ I have made a horseshoe shape out of the tail of the rope and am beginning to desensitize the areas around the head.

3/ This is about as tangled up as I can get one. The foal moved back to the other end of the pen, and the rope is running from the front leg, between the back legs, around the chest, and over the back. The foal has pretty well given up on the idea of fleeing at this point.

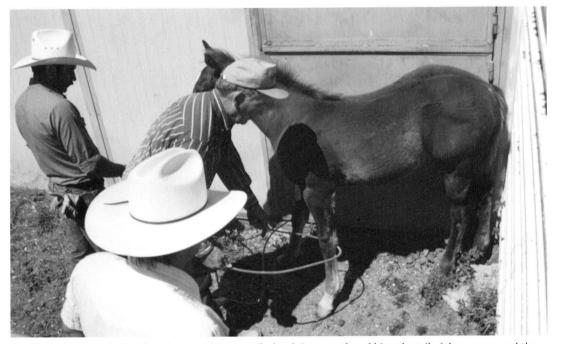

5/ The foal has been haltered, and an assistant is at the head. I am gently rubbing the tail of the rope around the foal's other front leg, the idea being to desensitize both sides of the body equally.

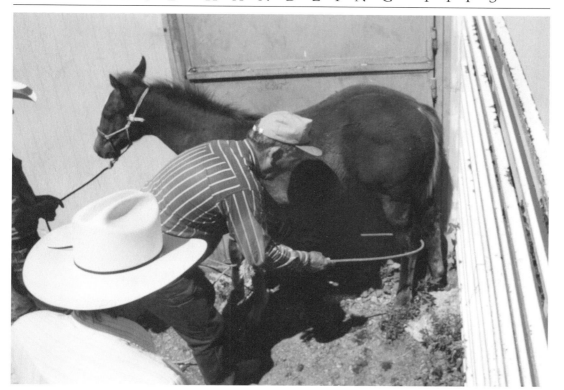

6/ *Rubbing the tail of the rope above the hock, directly on the hock, and just below the hock. I spent less than a minute working the rope like this in each of those areas.*

known to pull back while tied, or who want to run off while being led, those horses do not seem to exhibit that behavior anymore. And I have also noticed that afterwards, with foals, they seem easier to halter-break; and if a halter rope is dropped on a foal, it does not seem to scare him and make him run from it.

A couple more tips on trimming foals: If you do colts early in the morning, before it gets hot, they do a lot better. If they get hot and sweaty, it doesn't work as well as it does ordinarily. Everything is kept low-key and calm. I do not do a lot of talking around them, and I do not like anyone else "helping out" by hollering "whoa" all the time.

When I have the rope between the colt's hind legs, I rub it above the hocks, right on the hocks, then just below the hocks. When I am ready to pick up a hind foot, he will bring it right to me. When I put the rope over the top of his head, I rub it around the ears, take it off, put it on. I would say it feels to him like he is in captivity, but there is nothing around his throat, so he probably doesn't feel like he might be choked.

Finally, I cannot emphasize too much

7/ *Before picking up the hind foot by hand, I picked it up a couple times with the rope.*

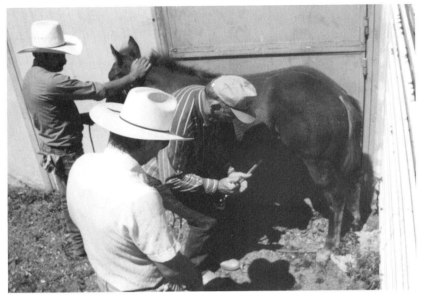

8/ I have already trimmed the front and back feet on the other side. I am working on the left front foot now, and the foal remains calm and relaxed.

9/ Before reaching down to pick up the back foot, I first got hold of the tail with one hand and twisted it slightly in a counterclockwise direction. I then picked up the foot with my other hand and released the tail. The tail-twist added insurance that the foal would not kick when I initially picked up the foot.

10/ The last foot is trimmed. The entire procedure on this foal took about 15 minutes from the time I walked into the pen with him.

the importance of safe working conditions—a small, smooth pen that a foal cannot get through or over. In the case of the older horse, it's important he be tied to something stout and with a smooth surface the horse cannot snag with a foot if he strikes during an initial struggle.

I mentioned earlier that I accidentally discovered The Short Rope Act when I was trying to trim an aged mare who was pretty rank. She was haltered and tied to a post, but would try to paw and strike at me when I tried to lift up a front foot. I got a loop around her foot, and was working to tie it up to her belly.

The loop slipped up above her knee in the process, and she was pawing and striking so badly that I sent a bystander off to find a piece of wire to make a hook to remove the rope. Before he got back with the wire, I was able to get the rope off the mare's leg. She had stopped and looked at me, and let me trim her foot, just like that. And that is when I figured out the whole deal.

Handling Mules

Mules who are well-broke are good to shoe. But a lot of mules are not that well-broke even though they are used for packing or riding and do pretty well for that type of work. A mule is different from a horse, not only physically, but mentally as well.

The old joke about striking a mule with a 2 by 4 to "first get his attention" is just that—a joke. But there is a measure of truth in another old joke about a mule "being your best friend for 20 years—just to get one good chance to kick your head off." The point is, one never wants to abuse a mule, because a mule will remember what you did to him, and he will get even with you at some point.

The good news: A mule will respond to The Short Rope Act the same as a horse. It might take a little longer for the mule to respond to it, but the result will be the

same. The procedure is the same. So if I have to shoe a mule who is not well-broke, I can get the job done with this method of handling, and not have to tie him up or abuse him in any way.

A side note on mules: Seldom will you ever find a mule who interferes. If he bumps himself, he will change his way of going so there is no chance of hurting himself again. For this reason, a mule seldom loses a shoe because his feet seldom bump one another. A mule may lose a shoe by getting it caught in something, but not from interfering.

Bad Horses

In bygone days, I have tied up a front leg, or tied up a back leg, or tied all four feet together to shoe a bronc lying on his side. I cannot see spending time discussing these procedures to any degree, because I really do feel they are pretty much outdated. Our knowledge of horse handling and training has progressed a lot through the years, to the point that we do not run across as many really bad horses as we used to. And The Short Rope Act really does replace these other methods.

A blindfold can still be put to good use on a horse who is bad about trying to cow-kick you with a hind leg when you reach down to pick up either a front or back hoof. The idea: With a blindfold on, he cannot see you to zero in on you.

But it is harder to work on a foot that is tied up. A front leg might be tied with a strap that encircles the forearm and

Our knowledge of horse handling and training has progressed a lot through the years, to the point that we do not run across as many really bad horses as we used to.

1/ *The Short Rope Act can be used successfully on older horses, and on donkeys and mules. The only difference is, on anything other than a foal, I prefer to have the animal haltered and tied securely. This is a young mare who has shown a tendency to kick. I want to get her over that idea so I can trim her feet. I do not expect her to react strongly to the rope around her legs initially—if I did, I would prefer that she be tied to a solid wall, so there would be no chance she could thrash around and get a leg through the fence. Note that the loop is around one of her front legs.*

2/ *I snugged the loop up, and she is not particularly bothered by it.*

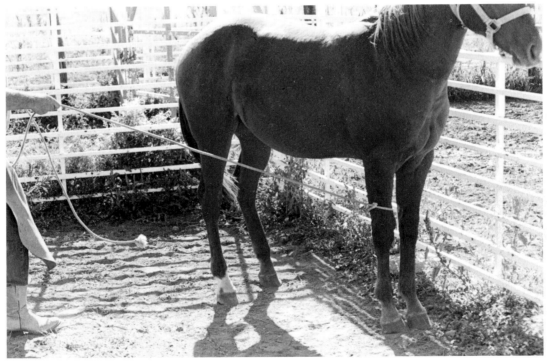

3/ I flip the tail of the rope around her back leg . . .

4/ . . . and pull it around, so that I now have the back leg "caught" as well as the front leg.

5/ I gave her a little time, and she soon lost interest in kicking with that back leg.

6/ I dropped the rope, moved back to the front leg, and then trimmed the front foot.

7/ I then moved to the hindquarters, picked up the hind foot . . .

8/ . . . and proceeded to trim it. Remember, each horse is still an individual. Some will need more time to cooperate than others.

pastern, or the horse might be saddled and a cotton rope attached to the saddle horn and tied around the pastern, holding the foot up. Or the back leg might be held up by being tied into the tail.

If a horse is used to being handled this way, however, you can sometimes get away from having to work on him with his foot tied up by first tying up the foot, then tying a handkerchief around his pastern. After a minute of that, you can untie the foot, leave the handkerchief in place, and quite often this type of horse will let you trim and shoe the foot. The

handkerchief makes the horse think his foot is still tied up. But don't forget to remove it when you are finished.

As for tying down a horse, that is not a good policy. Working such a horse first, riding him or longeing him, would probably be a much better idea. A tired horse is always easier to work on than one who is fresh. Besides, most people probably

9/ I used the same proce-
dure on this donkey who
seemed to need it, exhibit-
ing a tendency to kick.

10/ In this instance, I held the rope around his hind leg as I moved
under the foot to trim it.

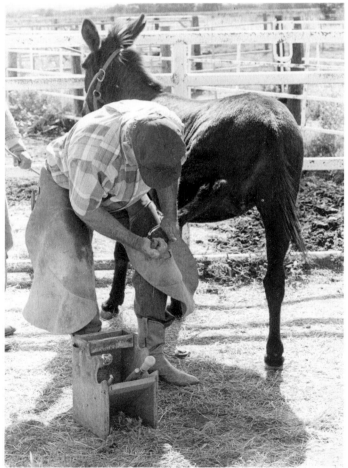

11/ This was about the third time I had trimmed this donkey, after
originally using The Short Rope Act on him. I was careful and took my
time picking up his feet, and had no trouble completing the trimming.

12/ *These young brood-mares, without foals at side, were easy to trim tied together in a pipe corral. They were used to being together, and—while they did not receive a lot of handling day in and day out—they stayed relaxed in each other's company.*

would not get all four feet tied securely enough to work on without getting pawed. If a horse who is tied down can get even one foot loose, especially a front foot, he can reach a long way to strike someone.

I think it is dangerous to try to shoe a horse who is either tranquilized or twitched.

When working on a tranquilized horse, there is a danger that he will suddenly emerge from his daze and jump into you, try to paw, or even bite. Even if the tranquilizer is working properly, the horse will be sleepy and hard to work on.

Horses who are frequently twitched on the nose for various reasons really start to hate the twitch. This type of horse will often try to paw while the twitch is being applied, and/or paw as the twitch is being released. A long-handled twitch is extra dangerous if it ever gets away from the person holding it. Invariably, if this happens, the horse will lunge into a person, rather than away from him, and that loosened twitch handle dangling from his

nose suddenly becomes a club. I have twitched some horses on the ear, by hand, and gotten along better than twitching them on the nose.

But the way I see it, if a horse really is an outlaw, a person can fool around with lip chains, war bridles, or the other things we have talked about, or he can take the horse to the auction barn. The latter is preferable. In defense of the horse, I do believe most bad horses are manmade. A horse who is really bad about his feet probably never had anyone competent try to trim or shoe him.

3

TOOLS OF THE TRADE

A good anvil will have different places on it to do different things to a shoe.

Anvil

A GOOD ANVIL is one of the first things you need to get as a horseshoer. The anvil is the main tool for shaping shoes. There are different anvils on the market, but the old anvils made back in the 1800s are still the best, in my opinion. There are still a lot of them around the country—they don't wear out—and if a person looks for them, he can find them. Some of the best were made by Haybudden and Peter Wright. Those old shop or farrier anvils have excellent steel in them. They were cast in two pieces, the top being steel, and the bottom a kind of draw-iron casting.

The best size of anvil is over 100 pounds. Anything that weighs less than that has a tendency to bounce around while you're working on it. A light anvil is hard to stabilize, and must be fastened down to the anvil stand in order to keep it

from crawling off the stand as you hammer on it to shape the shoes.

Anvil Stand

Finding the proper height of the anvil as it sits on the stand is also important. If the anvil is too high for you, you will hit with the heel of the hammer and put marks in your shoes. If the anvil is too low for you, you will hit with the front of the hammer and put marks in your shoes. Those marks are a sign of inefficiency.

The best way to determine height is to

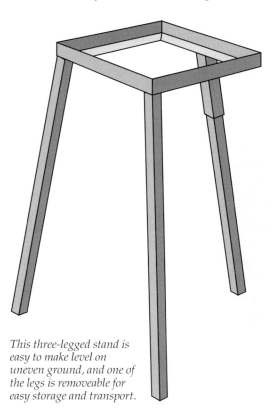

This three-legged stand is easy to make level on uneven ground, and one of the legs is removeable for easy storage and transport.

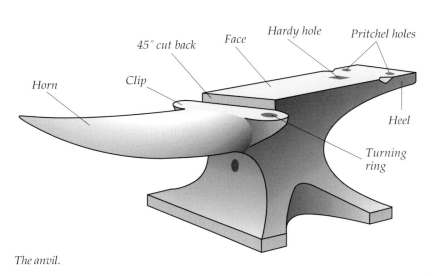

45° cut back   *Face*   *Hardy hole*   *Pritchel holes*

Horn   *Clip*

Heel

Turning ring

The anvil.

I do a lot of traveling in this lightweight pickup, which gets good gasoline mileage and has a covered bed with a lock on it. I can carry everything I need for my shoeing jobs in the back of this pickup, including the anvil (below). And if I have only one or two horses to shoe cold, I might not bother putting the anvil on the stand. I'll put it on the tailgate of the pickup, and let it rest on a thin, sturdy sheet of steel I carry along.

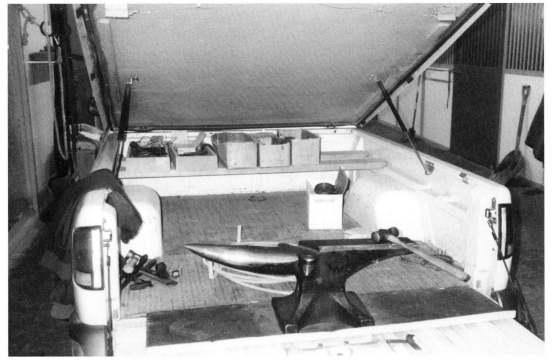

Turning cam—for turning branches on any hand-made shoe, while it is hot. A branch is put into the fork and held in place and turned by means of tongs and rounding hammer. This device fits into the hardy hole on anvil.

Forepunch—used to make nail holes in hand-made shoes.

Pritchel—used after the forepunch, to make finished nail holes in hand-made shoes.

stand next to it, with your shoulders squared. Take your rounding hammer, the hammer you used for shaping shoes, and hold it directly flat in front of you with the flat face of the hammer sitting on the heel of the anvil, perfectly square. That's how high your anvil should be.

I keep my anvils sitting on a little piece of cork on each corner of the stand. This gives the anvil some life. I can hammer all day on it and never get a sore elbow or shoulder—because it has a little give to it. If your anvil sits on a dead-flat surface, you will find you will be sore in the wrist, elbow, and shoulder at the end of a day.

A good steel anvil has a good ring to it. Sitting on cork (or on leather, or even little pieces of wood) also enhances the ring while preventing the anvil from hurting you. Some people believe a good, clear ring on the anvil will hurt their ears over time, but I have listened to the ring for over 50 years. I can still hear, and I have the ringing-est anvil in the business.

A good anvil will have different places on it to do different things to a shoe. When I straighten the branches of a shoe, I put it over the heel of the anvil and hit forward and down. I don't drive the shoe back toward me, I drive it away from me to get more stretch in the shoe.

There should be a ring or turning cam on the side of the anvil, for bending a shoe. On the anvil horn is where you round out the toe. You should learn the different places on the horn where you can slip the shoe to get different sizes. If I was a young man starting out in this business, I would take a lot of old shoes that someone else had fit, and see just where these

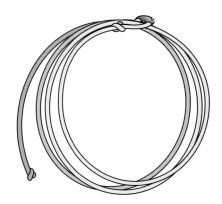

Every farrier should carry a nylon catch-rope.

different sizes of shoes would mark on the horn of my anvil.

Rounding Hammer

Rounding hammers are used to shape shoes on the anvil. Most of these hammers weigh from $1\frac{1}{2}$ to 2 pounds. Because we have a wide variety of factory-made shoes these days, there is very little adjustment that needs to be done to them, and most adjustment can be done cold, rather than hot. So this hammer is ideal for this type of work. However, you may have to do some adjustment work on the handle.

Many of the commercially made hammer handles are too heavy and too thick in the throat, which is the first 6 inches back from the hammer head. Using a handle like this feels like you're using a club—it's a dead hit, there is no spring to it, and it will not move steel the way it should.

I draw all these hammer handles down in the throat. I use a rasp to thin down the wooden handle, then smooth off the wood with glass—a broken pop bottle—which really does do an excellent job of smoothing. This lightens the handle, puts some spring into it, and I find I get a heavier hit with a handle like this.

The handle is more comfortable to hold after this alteration—my hand will slide right up to wherever the thickness of the handle is easiest to hold. One final alteration: Most manufactured handles are about 2 inches too long. That much handle usually needs some cut off to prevent the end of the handle from hitting the inside of my forearm as I use the hammer. These changes need to be made on the driving hammer as well as the rounding hammer.

Driving Hammer

This is the hammer used to drive nails through the shoes and hoofs. There are different weights to these hammers, but again, by thinning the handles on these hammers, you will find you have more life

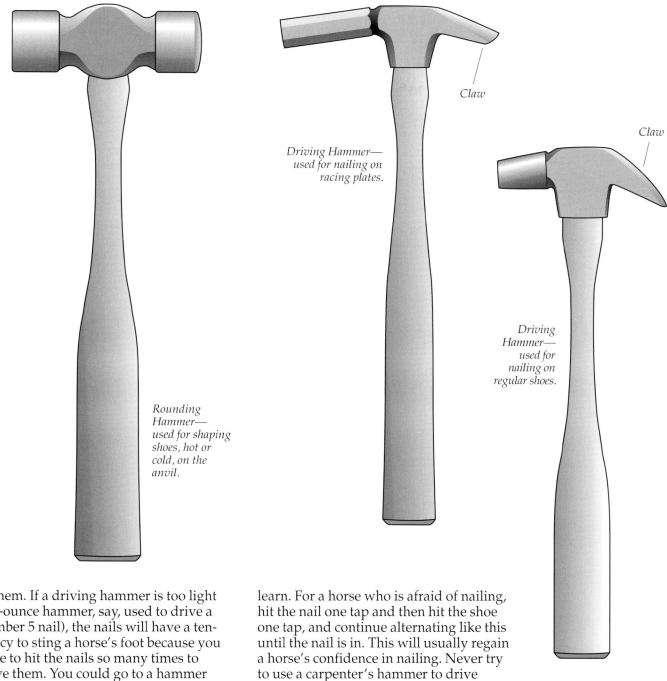

Rounding Hammer— used for shaping shoes, hot or cold, on the anvil.

Driving Hammer— used for nailing on racing plates.

Claw

Claw

Driving Hammer— used for nailing on regular shoes.

to them. If a driving hammer is too light (a 6-ounce hammer, say, used to drive a number 5 nail), the nails will have a tendency to sting a horse's foot because you have to hit the nails so many times to drive them. You could go to a hammer that is perhaps 3 to 6 ounces heavier and drive those same nails with ease.

Most of the time, when you have trouble nailing a shoe on a horse, it's because the horse is afraid of the nails. He probably got that way from someone using a hammer that was too light, or the shoer hit the nail too hard, bruising the horse's foot.

Finesse in driving a nail is important to

learn. For a horse who is afraid of nailing, hit the nail one tap and then hit the shoe one tap, and continue alternating like this until the nail is in. This will usually regain a horse's confidence in nailing. Never try to use a carpenter's hammer to drive horseshoe nails. Such a hammer is too heavy, and will likely scare the horse.

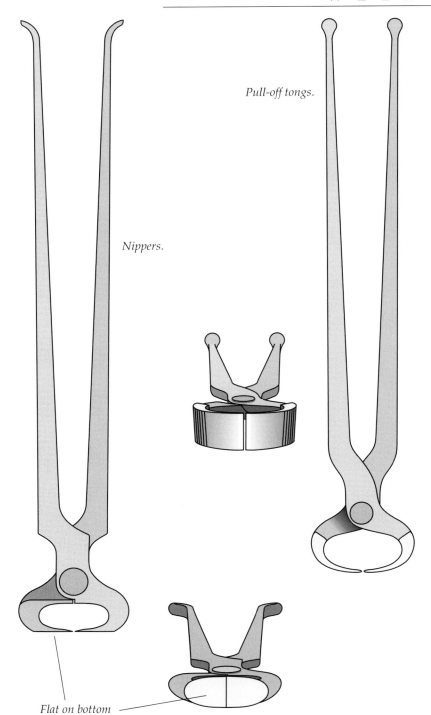

Pull-off tongs.

Nippers.

Flat on bottom

Nippers

There are several makers of nippers, which are used to nip off the horse's hoof. Prominent manufacturers of nippers and all other horseshoeing tools include GE (for George Ernest, the designer), DS (for Dale Sprout), and the Diamond Company. I have also used some real good nippers and other tools made by three California gentlemen from around 1940 to 1970. They included Harry German, John Burton, and a fellow named Kerseling.

Pull-Off Tongs

Pull-off tongs are used to pull off old shoes. They look similar to nippers. You work them under first one side of the shoe, then the other, apply leverage, and pull the shoe off. This tool can also serve other purposes. I use pull-off tongs that have a narrow jaw and a serrated edge so I can spread a shoe easily. This is handy. A lot of times a shoe is maybe 1/8- or 1/4-inch too narrow. Using this tong, I can open the shoe that much without getting out from under the horse and going back to the anvil. This makes for a very convenient tool. This tool will also pull a nail that is going in wrong, whereas the claw of your hammer might not be able to pull it out.

You can cut off the ends of your nails with these pull-off tongs. The way the blade is shaped, the cutting edge is set back in such a manner that it leaves the right length of nail to clinch down on the hoof. This tong will also open wide enough to clinch the nail down properly on the hoof. A clinch can then be finished neatly by using a serrated clinching tool called an alligator.

Learning to use these tools in the most efficient way can make the work easier.

Shoeing Stand

Many horseshoers use a stand to finish a horse's foot. Making this stand the proper height is important. You may have to lower or lengthen the legs of the stand several times to where it is most comfortable for you to finish a horse's feet.

I do not use a stand. I have feet on the bottom of my "stand," and it is always where I need it. When I tried to use a stand, it was always some place where I could not reach it without letting the foot down and getting the stand. So, I have learned to not use the stand, and feel it is best for people to not use a stand if they are physically able to hold up a horse's foot while finishing it. But I know a lot of shoers figure they can use the stand to be in more of an upright position, and they probably do a better job than they could without it.

Tool Box

Your hand-tool box—the box you carry your tools in while working on the horse—should be made in such a way that you can easily get your tools in and out of it while working under the horse. A lot of boxes I see are too tall. If a box is more than 12 or 14 inches tall, it is too tall to use comfortably, because a person will find he continually bumps and bruises his hand while reaching for tools. Most boxes need to be from 8 to 10 inches wide and a foot high. I like a sloping bottom in the box with the tool handles pointing out where I can reach them easily.

A tool box should also be made with a round tray in the top, where the nails will generally lie straight, and be easy to pick up. In a flat tray, nails will lie in every direction and are harder to pick up.

A word of caution here: Don't carry *too much* stuff in your tool box. A box that weighs 25 or 30 pounds or more is entirely too heavy to move from one foot to another. The main tools you need in the box are the nippers, pull-off tongs, hoof knife, alligator, driving hammer, and, of course, rasp and nails. If you can keep your box to less than 10 pounds, it will save you physically. But if the box is full of punches and cutters, and so on, it can weigh 30 or 40 pounds, and that turns into excessive work.

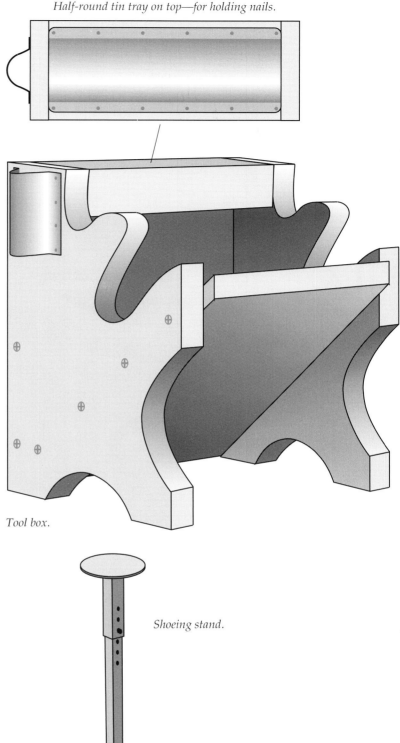

Half-round tin tray on top—for holding nails.

Tool box.

Shoeing stand.

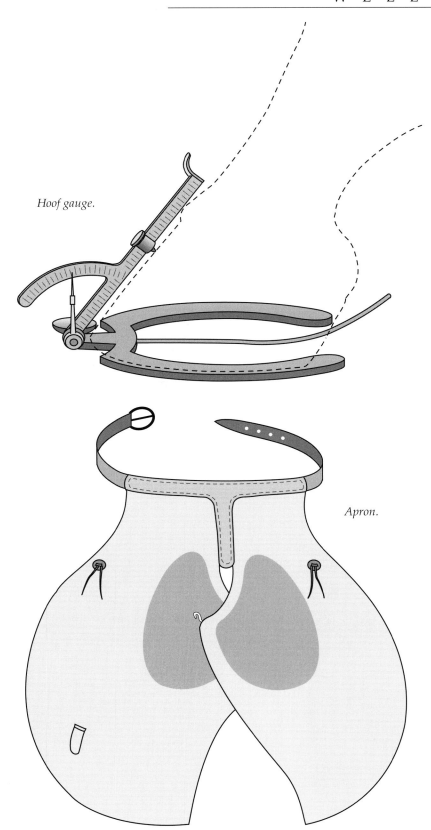

Hoof gauge.

Apron.

Hoof Gauge

If a person does not have a trained eye for figuring the angle of a horse's foot, he needs to carry a hoof gauge. You can build a little scaffold on the side of the tool box to carry the gauge (you can also make a holder on the side to carry a knife and sharpening file).

Apron

Another weight consideration is in your choice of apron. Some aprons are made of heavy leather, and can weigh perhaps 20 pounds. That much weight pulling on your hips throughout a day's work is very tiring. Use an apron made of lighter material and then use a little heavier patch in the appropriate places. The light leather is also cooler to work in.

Rasp

As for shoeing rasps, there are five or six companies that manufacture them. Years ago, a rasp would do probably 100 to 150 horses and still be reasonably sharp afterwards. But now most of these rasps are probably going to be fairly dull after 20 horses. I start out by using a new rasp just on the feet, until I notice the rasp is not cutting as rapidly as it was. At that time, I use it as a finishing rasp to clean under the nails, polish the edge of the foot, and polish down the nail clinches.

So, using a rasp like this, one can probably finish another 20 horses. In other words, a rasp is good for about 40 horses. Pushing a dull rasp is really hard work, and will not produce a smooth job. There is a tendency, with a dull rasp, to roll the end of the toe while rasping down a foot, and that creates a slight gap between the foot and the shoe.

The rasp is probably one of the most expensive tools you will use. It can cost up to $20, and if a shoer uses three or four of them a week, that runs into money.

Hoof Knife

A hoof knife is uniquely designed to pare away dead sole and frog from a hoof

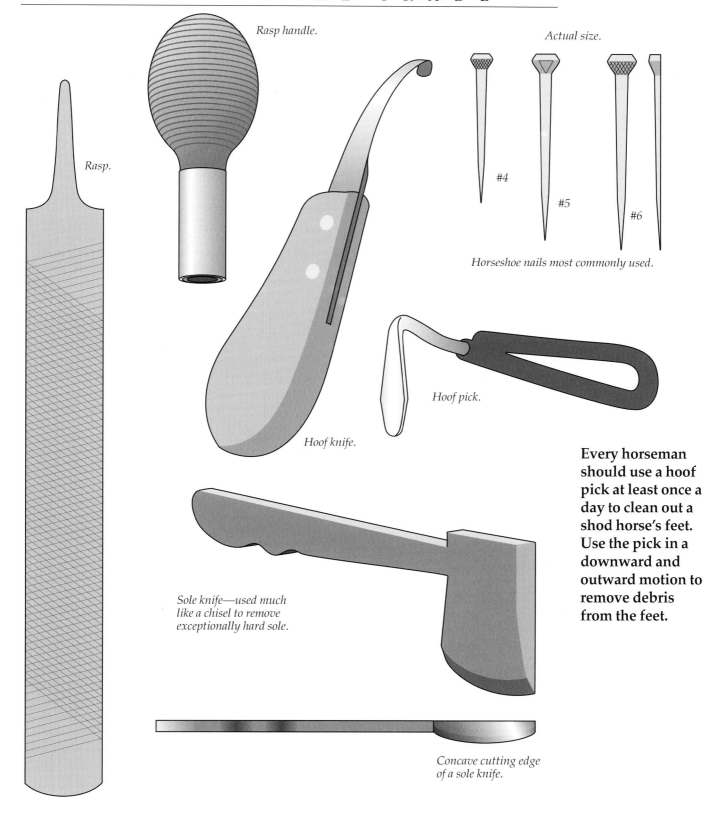

Rasp handle.

Actual size.

Rasp.

#4

#5

#6

Horseshoe nails most commonly used.

Hoof pick.

Hoof knife.

Every horseman should use a hoof pick at least once a day to clean out a shod horse's feet. Use the pick in a downward and outward motion to remove debris from the feet.

Sole knife—used much like a chisel to remove exceptionally hard sole.

Concave cutting edge of a sole knife.

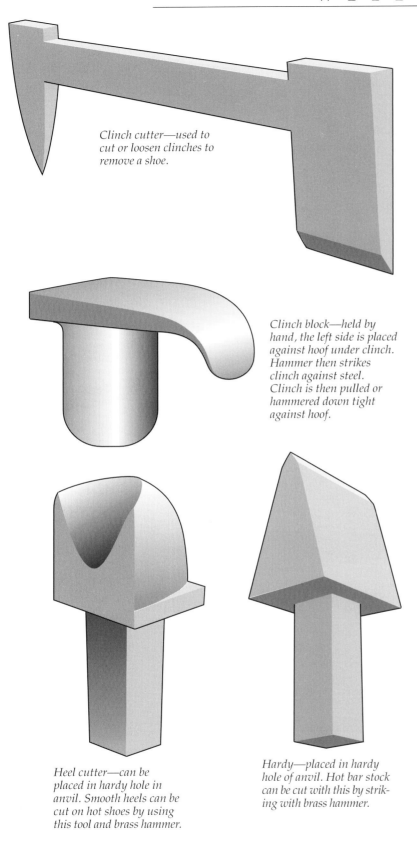

Clinch cutter—used to cut or loosen clinches to remove a shoe.

Clinch block—held by hand, the left side is placed against hoof under clinch. Hammer then strikes clinch against steel. Clinch is then pulled or hammered down tight against hoof.

Heel cutter—can be placed in hardy hole in anvil. Smooth heels can be cut on hot shoes by using this tool and brass hammer.

Hardy—placed in hardy hole of anvil. Hot bar stock can be cut with this by striking with brass hammer.

in preparation for shoeing. This tool has a wooden handle and thin blade with a hook at the end. These knives are made for left- and right-handed people, and the farrier supply store should carry both kinds. Every rasp has a special area at one end of it that is finely serrated for use in sharpening a hoof knife as it becomes dull from use.

Clinch Block

The clinch block should be used with discretion. Using it with too much force from the hammer can cause some problems. Therefore, I think it is generally best to not use a clinch block if the nails are driven properly and the nail heads are seated in the fullering (crease) of the shoe. About the only time I use a clinch block is on some horses who are going to be working in the feedlot or are going to the mountains, where those shoes really need to be tied on hard.

Problems related to the use of a clinch block can occur if the fullering isn't quite as deep as it needs to be on a shoe, and the nail head is sticking out. With the clinch block, the nail head will probably seat a little deeper in the fullering, but in doing so, there will be a lot of extra stress placed on the nail. Sometimes, there will be a hard place in a nail that will cause the nail to kink inside the hoof, when the clinch block is used, and this will sore the horse.

I find just pulling the nail down and making all the nails pretty equal with the pull-off tongs—cutting the nails to length—is about the best. And you will not run into the danger of clinching a horse too tight.

Forge

While most of today's shoeing can be done cold, there is still a need for a certain amount of custom work on forges. You can carry a portable forge, either gas or coal. I prefer a coal forge, mainly because you do not have to be as careful in hauling it in a pickup as you do in carrying a gas

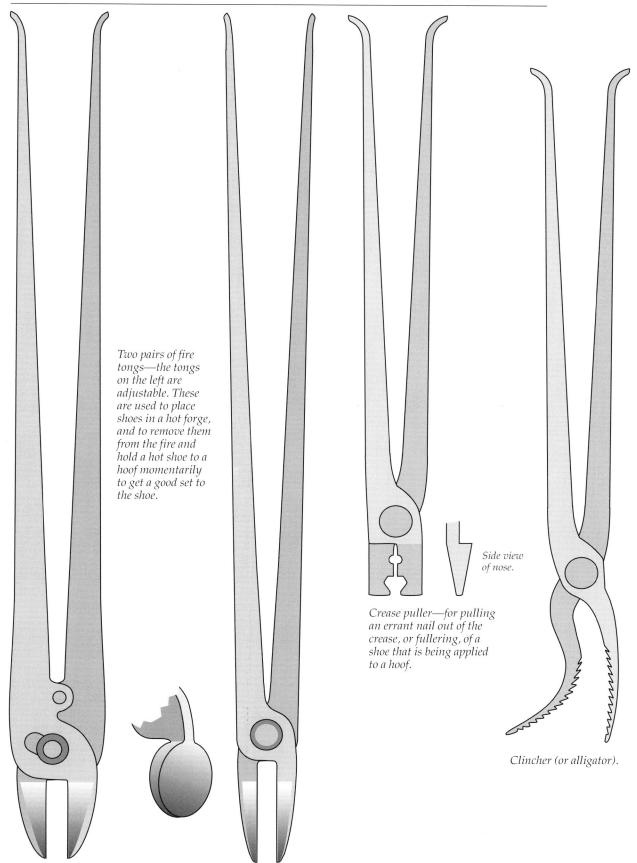

Two pairs of fire tongs—the tongs on the left are adjustable. These are used to place shoes in a hot forge, and to remove them from the fire and hold a hot shoe to a hoof momentarily to get a good set to the shoe.

Side view of nose.

Crease puller—for pulling an errant nail out of the crease, or fullering, of a shoe that is being applied to a hoof.

Clincher (or alligator).

more than likely have more coal than I will need on the trip.

Often, when I know ahead of time that I will need shoes fixed in a fire, I do the work at home. If I need a set of bar shoes, a set of shoes with trailers on them, calk shoes, or a shoe with a side clip, I can do this work at home. I remember the horses I will be working on, and very seldom does it take much adjustment to make specialty shoes to fit the horses. In this way, I can often be through shoeing a horse in the length of time it would take to set up the forge and get ready to do the work.

Keeping Yourself Comfortable

Good footwear on the person shoeing the horse is important. If a shoer's feet are comfortable, his back will stay comfortable, as a rule. If a horseshoer's back gets bad, most times it is from bad shoes. Same way with horses. If the horse's back is bad, sometimes that horse has been shod badly.

I have found that any of the athletic shoes, rubber-soled shoes, the neoprenes, and so forth give me more traction than I want. I prefer leather soles, a good arch, and heels made of rubber. With leather soles, it is easier to move your foot slightly, if necessary, while working on a horse, especially if you are working on asphalt or concrete.

With other types of soles, you can get "locked down" on the ground, and when that happens, a horse can lay into you or jerk and hurt you. A good arch really helps prevent stress-related injuries during those times when a horse moves over you, and puts maybe 500 or 600 pounds on your body.

Here's a tip for anyone who has a tendency to tie up in the back or suffer bad leg cramps from shoeing. The quickest way to relieve these conditions is to trot (jog) backwards. Trot about a block backwards and the tied-up muscles and tendons will be relieved. If you swing your arms while you are doing this backward exercise, this will also help sore shoulders.

Learning the proper stance while shoeing a horse is also important. Most shoers bend over too much, and will not swivel

A simple, efficient hot-shoeing operation in progress. The portable coal forge is set up on the tailgate of the pickup. The anvil on its stand is nearby, and so is a bucket of water.

forge that operates on butane. With bottled gas, a person naturally has to take extra precautions that the gas is securely transported, that hoses do not rupture, and valves do not vibrate open.

There is not much danger with a coal forge except when you have the fire built in it. A person can make his own forge—see the photos of mine, for example. When I go on the road for a week or so, I can take a 2½-gallon bucket of coal along, and their knees and bend their ankles to adjust to the height of the horse and still stay where the horse is comfortable holding his foot. A person can do more work working at the ends of his arms, instead of bent over and wadded up and working from the elbows to his waist. Learn to adjust in your knees and ankles.

Also, in this stance, think about keeping your butt down and your shoulders up. Continue to work at the end of your arms, and keep your tool against the horse's foot at all times. Do not "chop and jerk away" the excess hoof. Always use finesse. Chopping with the rasp or jerking with the nippers just causes more stress on your body.

Shoeing horses is one of the hardest jobs a person can do. You must be in good physical condition to shoe for a livelihood. A person in good condition should be able to shoe 15 or 20 horses a day. Some can do probably 30 a day. Most can do three or four in the morning and maybe four or five in the afternoon. But if there are 10 head to do, a person needs to stretch himself and set a pace to get through them and not overly exert himself.

If I have 20 horses to do, I set a pace to where I can have 10 done by noon. Maybe I will do one more if I am waiting for lunch to be ready. The point is, a horse-shoer needs to divide up his day for the amount of work he has scheduled.

Of course, if a guy has driving time between horses, that's a good time to get a little rest. But if a farrier will continue working instead of stopping to rest 5 or 10 minutes between horses, it will be easier to continue. When I finish a horse, I usually keep working while the owner goes to get the next horse. I go to the anvil and finish the shoes for the next horse. Or I sharpen a tool or something. If I stop and sit down and let my muscles tighten up between horses, I will be in trouble when I go back to work. I do not want my body to relax when I have to go back to work in a few minutes.

Keep water handy while working. Drink plenty of fluids, but I don't think soda pop does the job as well as water. Water will keep your system operating better than any other liquid.

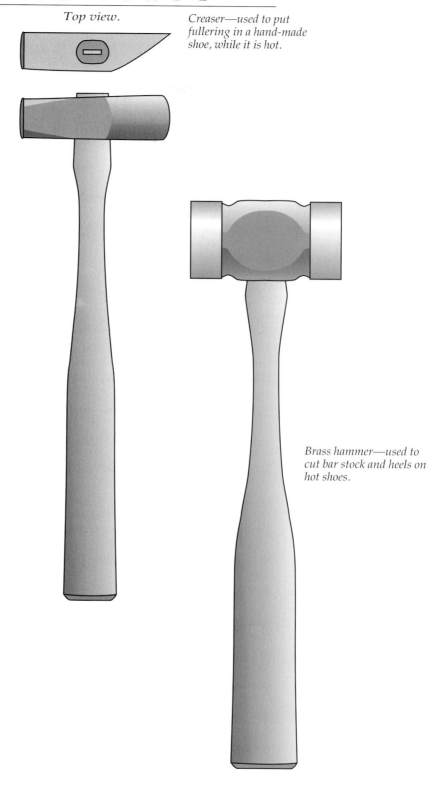

Top view.

Creaser—used to put fullering in a hand-made shoe, while it is hot.

Brass hammer—used to cut bar stock and heels on hot shoes.

4

BASIC TRIMMING

I lower nearly every horse's feet on the outside of the hoofs, in order to align the feet and keep them balanced.

MOST HORSES are better off if they can be left barefoot, rather than shod, especially if they are shod with ill-fitting shoes that stress their feet needlessly. A lot of horses used just for casual weekend riding on good ground can get along fine without shoes. With this type of light use, horses' feet toughen up so they can be ridden without getting sore.

To ride a horse right after he is trimmed is not wise, however, because his feet are soft where they were trimmed. But if a person will leave the horse alone for a day or two after he is trimmed, giving the hoofs time to dry and harden again, the horse can probably be ridden in this manner and require only a little trim every month to 6 weeks.

You will not need to cut any heel off a horse used like this. Just take a light cut with the nippers, cutting from the inside of the foot around to the outside (details to follow), and then roll the edges of each foot with the rasp. Lightly rasp off the excess shell that has grown. There is no need to cut off more than just a superficial amount of sole and frog, if that, on unshod horses because the sole and frog have been shedding away about every 30 days, as nature intended.

Rolling the edge of the foot with the rasp is very important. This takes the sharp edge off the foot, and will generally prevent the foot from chipping. If the rim of the foot is cut off to the sole line, seldom will you have any breakage there, because that part of the foot is good, live hoof.

Here's a test for a good healthy hoof, before you trim: Pick up a foot and see if there's a subtle flex in the hoof by squeezing it with your hands and knees. At the back of the frog, there is a slight crease that will flex closed and open as you apply and release pressure to the sides of the foot. If this flexibility in the hoof is present, that's a sign of a healthy hoof. The hoof probably has adequate moisture content, and the frog is soft enough so it is pumping blood back out of the foot and keeping the horse in a real normal state.

If there is no movement in the foot, the hoof is probably drier and harder than it should be. Perhaps applying a hoof dressing, or providing a constant puddle of mud at a water tank, would help correct the situation. If there is more than a slight motion in that little crease, that's a sign that the hoof may have a weakness, possibly a broken bar.

Most broken bars result from neglected feet that grew too long, and the horse picked up a rock and got it wedged in a foot. Sometimes a horse can break a bar by simply stepping down on a real sharp rock. But generally, horses with feet kept in good condition, and especially shod horses, will not break a bar in a foot. A broken bar can be mended, incidentally, and for more on that, see the chapter dealing with corrective shoeing.

When trimming and shoeing a horse, it is of utmost importance that the farrier know what he is doing in order to align the feet and keep them properly balanced. That is the basis for this book—to help the horse's movement, not hinder it.

I have found very few horses through the years who move with perfectly level feet, which is what most people say you need. I lower nearly every horse's feet on the outside of the hoofs, because the horse

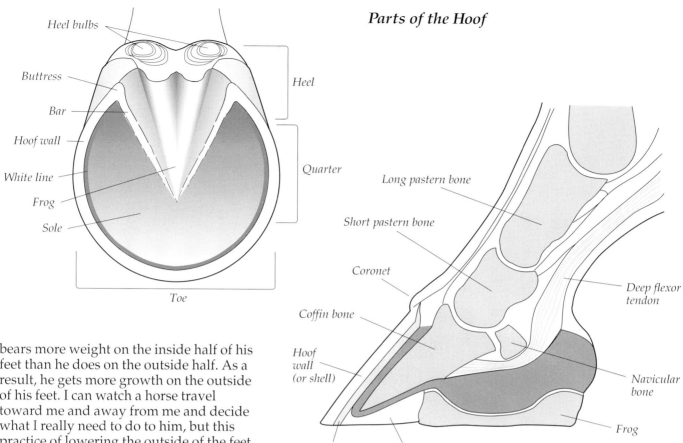

Parts of the Hoof

Heel bulbs

Buttress

Bar

Hoof wall

White line

Frog

Sole

Heel

Quarter

Toe

Long pastern bone

Short pastern bone

Coronet

Coffin bone

Hoof wall (or shell)

White line

Sole

Deep flexor tendon

Navicular bone

Frog

bears more weight on the inside half of his feet than he does on the outside half. As a result, he gets more growth on the outside of his feet. I can watch a horse travel toward me and away from me and decide what I really need to do to him, but this practice of lowering the outside of the feet slightly is pretty much a rule of thumb.

Having a horse aligned properly will make him ride a lot easier. If a horse is not aligned properly, his knees or ankles (fetlocks) will go in or out as his front legs move, and his hocks will likewise rotate awkwardly if he is out of alignment in his back legs. I try to fix the back feet to stabilize the hocks during movement. As I watch from behind, I *do* want the horse to cock his ankle slightly outward as he walks off. This is accomplished by lowering the outside of those hoofs, and the result is, when he stops, he will stop straight with his hind feet, and not splay them outward.

Sometimes it takes more than proper trimming to help correct these alignment problems, and that is where we resort to corrective shoeing. But there is a good chance a horse will avoid these problems altogether if he is put on a hoof trimming program as a foal.

A colt needs his feet trimmed when he is from 6 to 8 weeks old. When caring for a

baby like this, I generally just rasp the outside of the bottom of the feet and do not even touch the inside. The foal's neck is so relatively short at this stage of life compared to the length of his legs. Therefore, when he is grazing, he stands with his feet spraddled outward. He has a tendency to wear off the inside of his feet rapidly, causing him to splay out even worse. As soft as his bone structure is, if he spends a lot of time spread out eating in a pasture, he can wind up with crooked legs. I try to trim colts and fillies with a rasp twice before they are weaned at around 6 months of age.

I try not to start shoeing a horse until he is a 2-year-old or is broke, but a lot of times I have to shoe yearlings being shown in halter classes and horses who

51

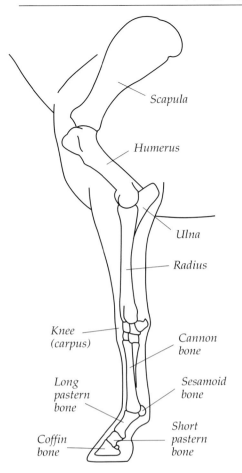

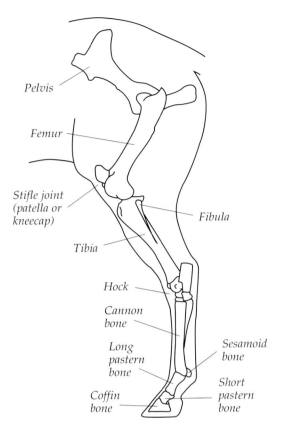

live where the ground is hard, gravelly, or rocky. But until a horse is 2 years old, his feet are still maturing, and it is best to let them go without shoes so they can spread and grow naturally. If a horse is constricted with shoes and not cared for at regular intervals, that's when there can be a lot of trouble with contracted heels.

I believe most horses have a tendency toward being "right-handed"—kind of like people. Therefore the right front foot takes more stress than the other front foot because horses move their weight onto that foot when they go into motion. The inside of the right front foot often shows more wear than on the left. And so the right front foot is really important to watch, because it has a tendency to toe out worse than the others. It is the more natural lead for many horses, and when a horse is standing at rest, the right front foot is most often tilted toward the right, ready to move off. One will generally find he can move a standing horse to the

left easier than to the right, because of the right front foot being out ahead of him.

On most performance horses I shoe, I trim to lower the outside of the feet. When those horses reach to get some ground, they do not have the stress they would if their feet were flat or high to the outside. This simple factor of lowering the outside really helps prevent ringbone and sidebone on cutting horses, roping horses, barrel horses, or other high-performance horses who work and pull hard in turns. Stress that comes from the outside of the foot is what creates nearly all the sidebones, ringbones, and soreness.

Trimming

There's only one difference in trimming a horse who is to be shod versus trimming a horse who will be left barefoot. With the horse to be shod, we need to pare away the old sole and frog with a hoof knife (see photos). We do this because a horse with shoes cannot adequately shed his sole and frog—the shoes restrict this natural occurrence. So, after the dead layers of sole and frog have been pared away, we are ready to trim the foot.

With the pared foot in hand, I get ready to trim by looking at the point of the frog in the bottom of the foot (see diagram next page). I look across the foot and imagine a plane 3/8ths of an inch higher across that part of the frog, from one sidewall of the hoof to the other. By finding this point, I know how much foot to trim off with the nippers.

Keeping in mind the imaginary 3/8-inch plane over the point of the frog, I begin with the nippers about 1/4th inch higher than the ends of the buttress, back at the heel area. By starting at the inside heel, I can run my nippers on a slightly sloping imaginary line so I am at the 3/8ths plane by the time I am nipping away at the hoof adjacent to the point of the frog.

When I cross the halfway point of the hoof, in the middle of the toe, that's where I begin slightly lowering the outside hoof, and this measurement is relative. You can put the foot down and determine how much additional hoof needs to be removed on the outside to help align the foot. A lot of times, I will drop this foot straight down and see that it still sticks out a little to the side. I can pick it up, take a couple swipes with the rasp, and then drop the foot again and see that it is aligned straight forward.

Aligning the feet like this is important, even for horses who will not be shod. And with a couple swipes of the rasp—it does not take very much—a horse's foot can be realigned a half-inch to an inch, so it now faces straight forward instead of to the side.

With a sharp rasp, a person does not need to press down when lowering this outside shell of the hoof—a couple of light passes with the rasp, *rasping from the inside of the foot to the outside,* is all it takes. Use caution in rasping. It is easy to rasp off more hoof than you want.

The rasp is about 16 inches long, and when you go clear across the foot with it, using the coarse side, it is possible to remove from 1/16th to 1/8th of an inch, just in one swipe. Use the rasp to make a pass or two over the bottom of the entire foot, then float it once or twice over the outside half, for lowering that area, then turn the rasp over and use the soft side for one pass.

For a horse who is just being trimmed, not shod, you can roll the edge of the hoof from the bottom, without taking the foot out in front of yourself and rolling it from the top, down. Remember that rolling the edge of the hoofs like this is just for a horse who will not be getting shoes.

These dimensions—staying 3/8-inch higher across the plane of the foot at the point of the frog—will measure 1 inch from the point of the frog to the white line. And the shell of the hoof at that angle will be 3/8ths of an inch thick. These measurements will be the same on all breeds of horses, including ponies and draft horses.

Most horses, unless they have had a foot injury of some kind that distorted a foot, will work well when trimmed to these dimensions. Their feet are so very much alike, other than being different sizes. A colt generally has to become a yearling before these dimensions will work on him, but soon after, these measurements will work on about 95 percent of the horses.

Trimming in this fashion will make a toe 3½ to 3¼ inches long. That is a good foot on most horses people are riding these days.

This will also give that foot about a 50-degree angle. I try to shoe most horses at a 50- to 52-degree angle in front, and the back feet about 2 degrees steeper. So, going to the back feet, if the horse is at 50 degrees in front, I will make him 52 degrees in back—unless this is a reining horse. In that case I put on a sliding plate and shoe 2 degrees the other way in back. But more on that later.

The old cavalry horseshoeing manual advised cutting the hoof to a 45-degree angle. In all my practice, only on some gaited horses with wedge pads did I ever

Trimming Guidelines

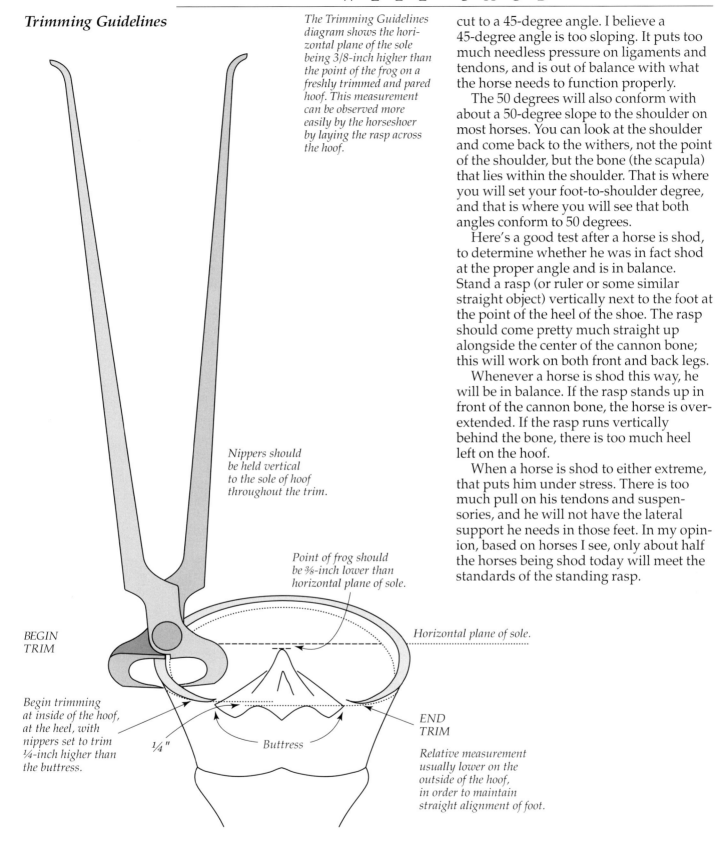

The Trimming Guidelines diagram shows the horizontal plane of the sole being 3/8-inch higher than the point of the frog on a freshly trimmed and pared hoof. This measurement can be observed more easily by the horseshoer by laying the rasp across the hoof.

Nippers should be held vertical to the sole of hoof throughout the trim.

Point of frog should be ⅜-inch lower than horizontal plane of sole.

Horizontal plane of sole.

BEGIN
TRIM

Begin trimming at inside of the hoof, at the heel, with nippers set to trim ¼-inch higher than the buttress.

¼ "

Buttress

END
TRIM

Relative measurement usually lower on the outside of the hoof, in order to maintain straight alignment of foot.

cut to a 45-degree angle. I believe a 45-degree angle is too sloping. It puts too much needless pressure on ligaments and tendons, and is out of balance with what the horse needs to function properly.

The 50 degrees will also conform with about a 50-degree slope to the shoulder on most horses. You can look at the shoulder and come back to the withers, not the point of the shoulder, but the bone (the scapula) that lies within the shoulder. That is where you will set your foot-to-shoulder degree, and that is where you will see that both angles conform to 50 degrees.

Here's a good test after a horse is shod, to determine whether he was in fact shod at the proper angle and is in balance. Stand a rasp (or ruler or some similar straight object) vertically next to the foot at the point of the heel of the shoe. The rasp should come pretty much straight up alongside the center of the cannon bone; this will work on both front and back legs.

Whenever a horse is shod this way, he will be in balance. If the rasp stands up in front of the cannon bone, the horse is over-extended. If the rasp runs vertically behind the bone, there is too much heel left on the hoof.

When a horse is shod to either extreme, that puts him under stress. There is too much pull on his tendons and suspensories, and he will not have the lateral support he needs in those feet. In my opinion, based on horses I see, only about half the horses being shod today will meet the standards of the standing rasp.

This hind foot has just been trimmed, after wearing shoes for about 10 weeks. My left hand is holding the portion of hoof that has been trimmed off with the nippers. Note that the sole and frog have been pared down with the hoof knife just enough to expose clean, healthy tissue.

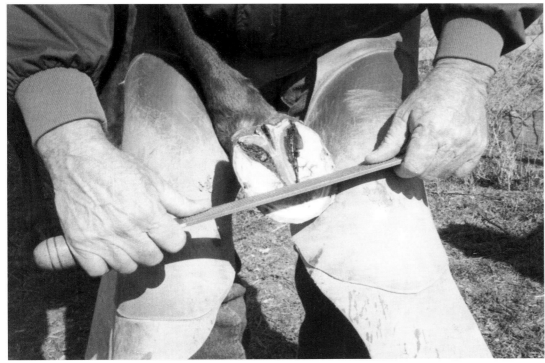

The point of the frog should be about 3/8-inch lower than the rasp.

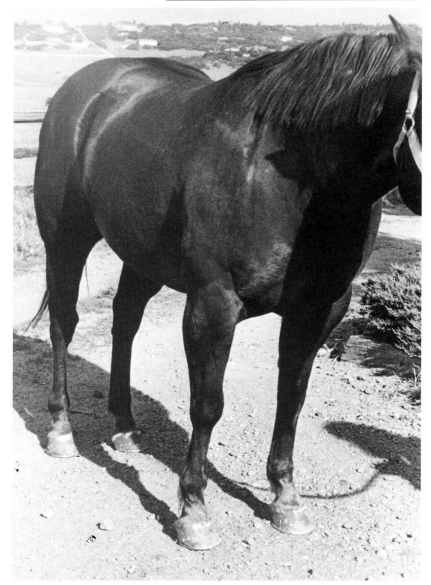

A horseshoer should always do his best to trim and/or shoe a horse so that the feet are aligned—in other words, do not toe in or out, but stay straight. Naturally, a horse with one or more crooked legs will not wind up with perfectly straight feet after he has been trimmed, but a farrier can often help such a situation with proper trimming. This horse shows good alignment with straight legs and feet right after being shod.

Some Anomalies

There are a few things a little out of the ordinary to be encountered when trimming horses. For example, some horses have a little pinpoint artery that runs out to the end of their toe or toes. I have seen it on all four feet of some horses, and believe it is generally caused by letting the horse go too long between shoeings, especially if the horse is kept shod constantly. The foot will typically be contracted, and there will be a slight bow in the sole of the foot. Anyway, running the rasp over the toe in a foot like this will cause bleeding, sometimes profuse bleeding.

The bleeding will stop in a little while—it really doesn't hurt anything. If I am shoeing the horse, I put the shoe on, but I put a little oakum (loose, stringy hemp fiber, used as calking material) over the source of the blood as I put on the shoe, because the bleeding will usually increase during the nailing. The oakum prevents blood from splashing around. It is good to try to get that foot to "open up," and maybe the little artery will recede back up the foot. More on opening up a foot in the chapter on corrective shoeing.

A double sole in a horse's foot is something else encountered from time to time. This is caused, generally, from an abscess in the foot, or a bad bruise in the foot, and the result will be a sole and frog connected and not shed normally.

Sometimes, there will be partial separation between the two soles, and you can remove them together or one at a time. The whole mass tends to separate and come loose as you work on the foot, paring down the sole and frog. The foot is usually excessively long, so the double sole can be removed entirely at that time, and one can see the fresh, new sole and frog under there. It will be the cleanest, brightest foot you've ever seen.

Sometimes, a horse will look real flat-footed, as if the frog and sole are completely flat in the bottom of the horse's foot. As a rule, all four feet will look the same, and this is typically caused by feet

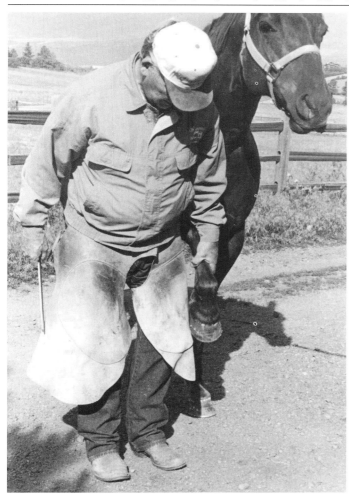

A good test to see if a horse's foot is aligning straight is to pick it up (left), then drop it. See how the foot lands. Does it land straight or toe in or toe out? This foot landed straight (right) when I dropped it.

that have been very hard and were not pared down adequately in the sole and frog for two or three shoeings. Several days of moisture will help feet like this so they shed themselves of this old frog and sole. The farrier can help the process by paring it all out.

Some farriers think this must be done gradually, but I have found if the foot is in the right condition and is trying to shed anyway, it is good to get it all cleaned out at once. One note of caution: Be careful a plug of hoof does not get pulled out of the foot. This would happen on a horse who had seedy toe—damaged laminae, common in horses who have foundered.

By paring out the sole, you can put a cup back in the foot and get it to growing normally again. Seldom do we get any soreness in a foot by cleaning it out and paring the bars and frog and soles out. Generally, in the time it takes to work on a foot like this, the foot will have opened up 3/8 inch or 1/2 inch. If that happens, I know the horse's foot is going to be a lot healthier now that it does not have all that restriction to it.

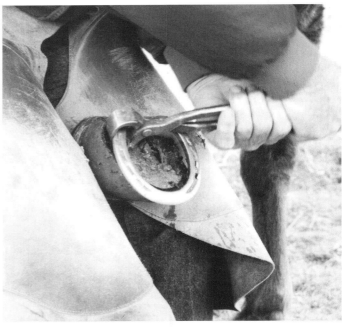

1/ This sequence of photos shows the left front foot being trimmed. We will begin by removing the shoe. The pull-off tongs are clamped between the shoe and hoof, and I work the tool from left to right to pull the shoe loose on that side. Note that the foot is held and supported firmly between my knees.

2/ The pull-off tongs are slipped under the other side of the shoe and closed. By rocking the tongs from side to side a few times, the shoe is now loosened on both sides . . .

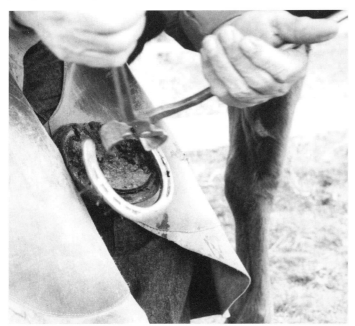

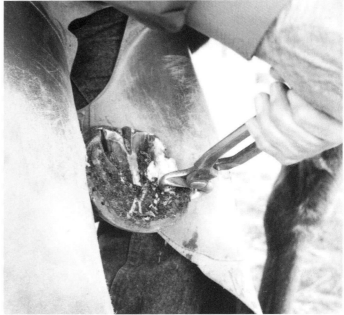

3/ . . . and it falls free. The nails have all pulled through the hoof wall (or shell), and remain in the shoe. The idea is to not break off a nail within the hoof, but to get all the nails to pull through the hoof and come off with the shoe. I will now use a hoof pick to scrape away the remaining dirt.

4/ This hoof has enough of a "cup" in it (meaning the sole is lower than the hoof wall) that I can simply proceed with the trimming. But I will use the hoof knife to clear away some of the dead sole and frog before I am finished. A hoof often needs to have the sole pared down a little initially in order to get a bite with the nippers. When using the nippers, always begin trimming at the inside of the hoof (the side closest to the opposite leg) near the heel. Note that just prior to beginning the hoof trimming on the wall of the hoof, I nipped away some old growth around the frog. This will make it easier to finish that job later with the hoof knife, when I pare away more frog and sole.

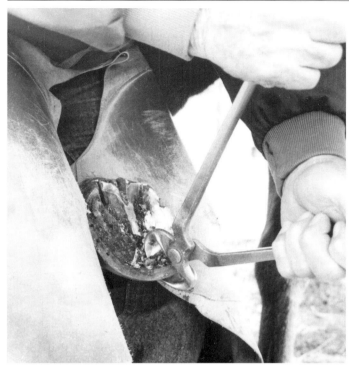

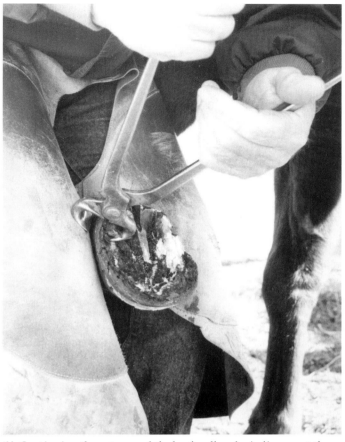

5/ I keep the nippers perpendicular to the sole of the hoof, and continue trimming around the hoof, from the inside to the outside. When I get to the toe of the hoof, I will increase the amount of bite the nippers take so that the outside of the hoof is slightly lower than the inside. This measurement is only a fraction of an inch, and it is relative. If more outside hoof needs to be removed in order for the foot to be aligned, a swipe or two with the rasp will do it. Take off a little at a time.

6/ Continuing the cut around the hoof wall and winding up at the outside heel, the trimming will often fall away in one piece.

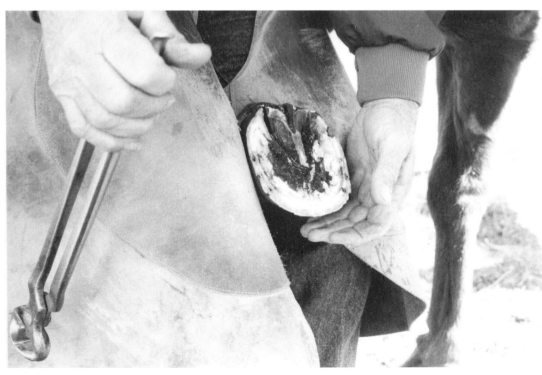

7/ This is what a healthy hoof looks like at this point. I will now pare away a little more of the sole and frog with the hoof knife.

8/ *Hoof knives are made for left- and right-handed people. The idea is to follow the natural contours of the sole, frog, and bars, paring away dead tissue, and going just deep enough so that good, clean tissue is visible.*

9/ *A few even swipes with the rasp, held flat against the bottom of the hoof, will nearly finish the job. I am using the fine side of the rasp here, because I do not want to really rasp away more hoof, I just want to smooth it.*

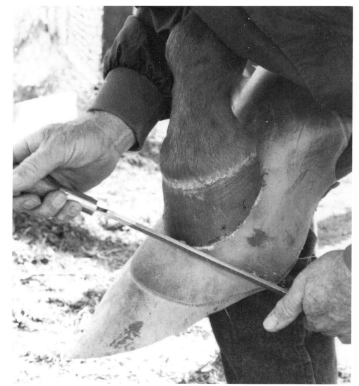

10/ *Rolling the edge of the hoof is important for a horse who will be going barefoot, as this one will. This helps prevent chipping of the hoof. If the horse is getting new shoes, this would not be done. To roll the hoof, the fine side of the rasp is lightly "rolled" over the entire edge, from one side to the other. Note that the foot has been between my knees, but I am now facing the same direction the horse is facing, and his foot is resting on my knee.*

11/ *I have repositioned the foot and the rasp to better roll the inside edge of the hoof.*

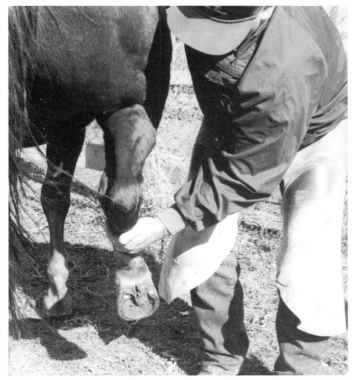

1/ Same horse, another foot. This happens to be the right hind. With my right hand on the horse's hip, I have just moved my left hand down his leg to pick it up.

2/ The horse's hoof is positioned between my knees in this fashion . . .

3/ . . . and comes to rest so I can begin work.

4/ *I reach into my tool box for the pull-off tongs, to remove the shoe.*

5/ *The hind shoe is removed in the same fashion as the front shoe.*

6/ *Notice how the foot is supported between my knees when I work the pull-off tongs from side to side.*

7/ This photo, and the following two photos, show how I can use the hoof nippers to begin trimming away dead tissue around the sole and frog.

9/ A little of the sole was cut away with the nippers, too, and this will make it easier to get a bite on the surrounding hoof wall with the nippers. After trimming, I will pare away the rest of the dead areas with the hoof knife, so that clean, bright frog and sole are exposed.

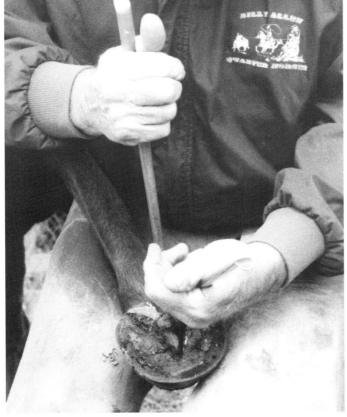

8/ I begin by working on the frog, moving down to the point of the frog. Notice the clean tissue that appears in the frog where I have nipped it away.

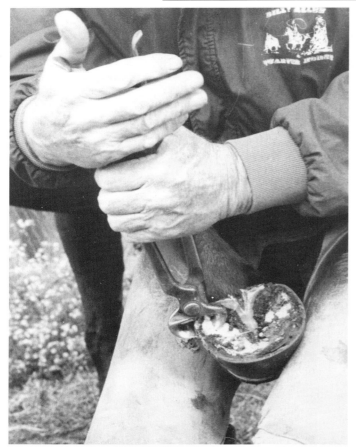

10/ *Because this is the horse's right hind foot, I begin trimming on the opposite side I started trimming when I was doing the horse's left front and back feet.*

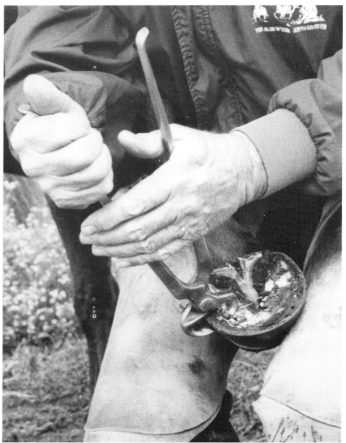

11/ *Trimming was started on the inside of the foot, and I am working the nippers down toward the toe. Following trimming with the nippers, the foot will be pared and rasped as it was on the front foot.*

Mares, Foals, and Stallions

I generally like to trim broodmares three times a year. I do most of them around the first of the year, then after they foal and the colts are on the ground, 6 or 8 weeks old. At that time I trim both the mares and the colts. If a colt has a crooked leg, I can trim him and try to get it straightened at that time. After the foals are weaned, I trim them and the broodmares again.

I will not trim a broodmare if she is within 30 days of foaling. I might trim her front feet, but there is no way I will trim her hind feet. Lifting the hind legs on a mare at that time will stress her, and trimming might make her feet sore. The stress might cause her to foal prematurely.

Most broodmares are pretty good to work on, especially if a group of them are all tied to a stout pipe fence in a corral.

When mares and foals are used to being together in a herd, it doesn't make sense to completely separate them from the others. The only reason for taking a mare and foal outside the corral for trimming would be to proceed with The Short Rope Act. But for the trimmings that follow, they can all be done together with the mares standing tied to the fence and their foals nearby. If the foals are being halter-broke at that time, they can easily be caught and trimmed while standing next to their mothers.

Most broodmares have a tendency to get what we call wide oval feet. Because they are so heavy on their feet, their feet spread out. I trim most of them by leaving some toe and taking off the sidewall, at an angle from the bottom of the foot. Then I roll the edges of the foot to give the foot some shape. If a person just takes all the toe off, then the foot will be wider than it is long, and the mare will be extremely sore-footed.

There are some mares who get so heavy in front that they need shoes on the front feet. Without shoes, heavy mares might

 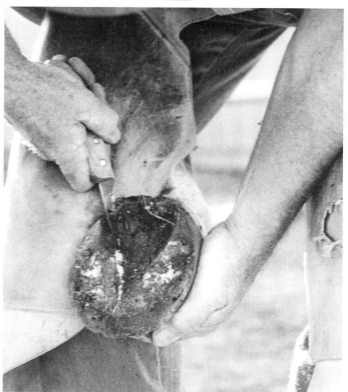

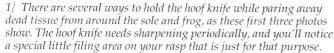

1/ *There are several ways to hold the hoof knife while paring away dead tissue from around the sole and frog, as these first three photos show. The hoof knife needs sharpening periodically, and you'll notice a special little filing area on your rasp that is just for that purpose.*

2/ *I am working on the horse's right front foot.*

get sore and stressed, and then founder. I seldom shoe the back feet on some broodmares because they are bad about kicking. They get cranky when they have babies. Also, unshod back feet are not as dangerous if a mare kicks at the stallion when being bred.

While we are discussing broodmares, I will pass along a tip. I have been to several places while foals were being born, and have helped deliver a few of them. I have observed foals who are pinched up—very close in the chest, and maybe are knock-kneed and toed out severely in front. They are weak and have a hard time straightening up.

One thing that might help a foal like that, I have found, is to make a "log roll" out of four or five old gunnysacks (or similar material). Put this log roll between the foal's front legs, right against his chest, and tie it around his neck and around his front girth area with some stout string. Stay with him till he quits pawing and fussing, and gets used to it. Then let him wear it for about 24 hours. At that time,

the roll can be removed, and there is a good possibility the colt will have spread in the chest and his legs have straightened out. I have seen this work a number of times, and highly recommend it.

I think imprint training (a *Western Horseman* book, *Imprint Training* by Dr. Robert M. Miller), in which a newborn foal is gently rubbed and handled all over his body, is a very good practice. Generally, I believe if a foal is touched and petted and handled the first 5 days of his life, he will not be a problem when handled and trained later.

In the country I travel, most of my customers' stallions are pasture-bred. On those stallions, I trim their feet but do not shoe them. A barefoot stallion will not injure the mare's back with shoes while servicing her.

If a stallion is kept in a stall and run, however, he will probably have to be shod because he will invariably run the fence, and wear his feet excessively without shoes.

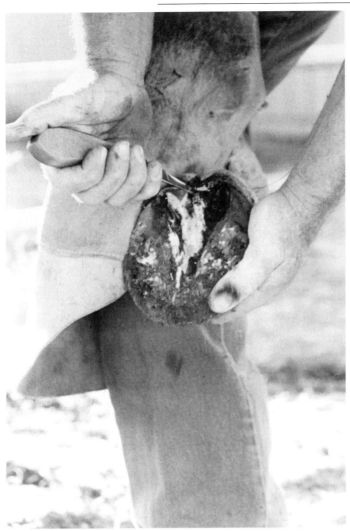

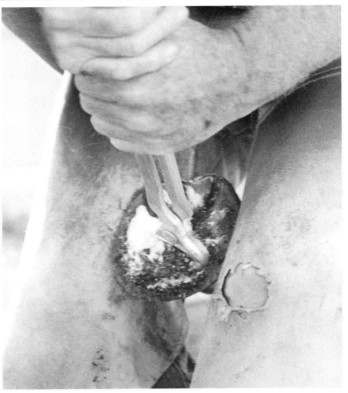

4/ Use of the hoof nippers can speed up the paring away of frog and sole. Here, I am using the nippers to dig into the dead sole. Remember, this horse just had his shoes pulled, and because he was wearing shoes, the soles and frogs were restricted, and the natural shedding of dead material in those areas was inhibited.

3/ Notice the clean, bright tissue begin to appear on the frog as the dead tissue is pared away.

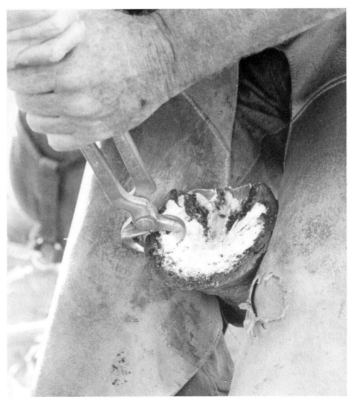

5/ This foot has been pretty well cleaned up with the hoof knife and nippers. There is a slight cup in the sole area, enabling me to use the hoof nippers now to trim away the hoof wall, or shell.

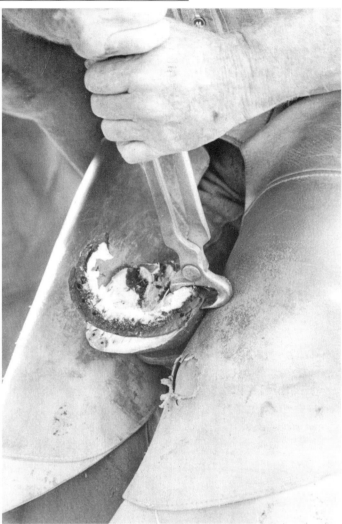

6/ *Working the nippers down toward the toe . . .*

7/ *. . . and finishing up on the outside of the hoof. The clipping is coming off in one piece.*

After a foot has been trimmed, remember to use caution in rasping. It is easy to rasp off more hoof than you want.

5 BASIC SHOEING

I try to shoe every horse symmetrically on his front feet, and symmetrically on his back feet.

BASIC SHOEING, for our purposes here, will deal with shoeing a saddle horse by means of the cold shoeing method as opposed to hot shoeing, in which a forge is used to heat the shoes and shape them more easily with hammer and anvil for a good fit. There is still a need for farriers to be able to work at a forge to build shoes or customize shoes for corrective purposes, and we will get into hot shoeing later. But with all the shoes that are on the market now, the cold shoe is just as good as the hot shoe for most purposes. These shoes have been designed with adequate length, and preshaped to the point where they need only a little adjustment with hammer and anvil in order to fit most every kind of

horse a shoer will encounter.

With the cold shoe, one has to be a little more precise at rasping the foot and getting the foot flat. With a hot shoe, the shoe will burn slightly into the foot, assuring a good tight fit. And with the hot shoe you can trim the heels of the shoe precisely to the length desired, where with the cold shoe, you may be $\frac{1}{8}$-inch long on the heels. But as a rule, cold shoeing is faster and easier than hot shoeing, and works just as well as hot shoeing. One of the main reasons for using the hot shoe: it is easier to move iron—to roll the toe of a shoe, or pull side clips, or turn heel calks. Still, a farrier can do a lot of these things cold if he has a good anvil and a hammer big enough to move iron.

I prefer the mild steel shoe to the drop-forge shoe. The drop-forge shoe (made from heated metal, pressed between dies) is harder and will not wear as quickly as the mild steel shoe, and for this reason it is a good shoe to use on horses who go to the mountains or rocks, places where a horse needs a little harder and longer-lasting shoe. The mild steel shoe (made from steel that is tough but malleable) has a tendency to wear in the toe a little more, but it will also open up with the horse's foot. On the other hand, the drop-forge shoe has a tendency to be so hard that the foot will crawl over the edge of the shoe, rather than expand as the hoof grows between shoeings. A shoe that can expand a little with the hoof is preferable for the horses I shoe—show horses and horses who do pretty precise work.

Most of the drop-forge shoes are made by Diamond, St. Croix, Breckenridge, and

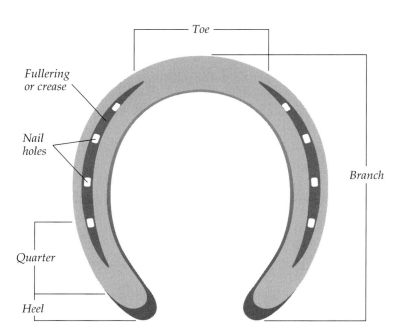

A typical manufactured shoe.

Nordic, and some of the Mexican shoes are the drop-forge version. The Kerck-haerts, the Deltas, Equine Forge, and the Isumi Japanese shoes are the most popular mild steel shoes on the market. I use some of all of them.

Years ago, we had to make everything we thought a horse might need. Now, we can order wide-web shoes, rim shoes, nearly any kind of shoe we need. Most of the supply houses are carrying heart bar shoes, aluminum shoes, aluminum bar shoes.

Some observations: I have found with aluminum shoes that some horses are allergic to them. You can pull off the shoe and find a thrush-like substance that has built up under it. And there will be deteri-oration and corrosion around the nails a lot of times with aluminum shoes. I also find with a lot of the rim shoes, I can get along good with them on front feet, but not on back feet. A rim shoe makes a horse reach farther with the foot, and whenever I have shod a horse behind with a rim shoe, it has made him reach and hit the bulb of the heel or the inside of the front foot. So I rec-ommend using a flat shoe on a horse behind, with just plain fullering.

I try to shoe every horse symmetrically on his front feet, and do the same thing to every front shoe whether it is an 0, 00, 1, 2, or whatever size shoe it is. The same applies to the back feet. By cultivating these feet to be the same size and shape, I am helping the horse to have the best possible balance. He will be able to use himself better than he could with a straight side, or narrow side, or heel pulled under one of those shoes. I also like to shoe a horse with a full heel on the shoe, one that comes back to the bulb of his foot. Most people think that leaving the heel a little long on a shoe is con-ducive to having that shoe pulled off, but that isn't so. The horse who pulls off a front shoe is generally forging, and hits that front shoe in motion with the hind foot, thereby shearing off the nails and knocking off the shoe. For a horse known to forge, the chances of that happening can be greatly reduced by shoeing with a square-toed shoe in back. I probably lose only a few shoes a year, but when it hap-

Toe

Squared toe on a hind shoe

The farrier puts the squareness in the toe by working the shoe with hammer and anvil.

pens, it is usually because a horse got into a fence or something that hooked the shoe and pulled it off.

Shaping the Shoe

After a horse has had his feet properly trimmed and pared down (Chapter 3), he is ready to be shod. At this point, the proper size shoes must be selected and then altered just enough to fit that individual horse.

For most horses, it takes two sizes of shoes to fit them. If one is shoeing a horse with a real symmetrical front foot, as a rule that front foot will be a size larger than his hind foot, unless the horse is wearing a slide plate or a longer shoe for reining on the back. So, to just buy a set of number 1 shoes, or 5 or 6 shoes, or what-ever, will not work out too well most of the time.

Most of the shoes on the market, as I said, are pretty well shaped symmetrically, but one thing the manufacturers do needs correcting: They leave the toe a little bit

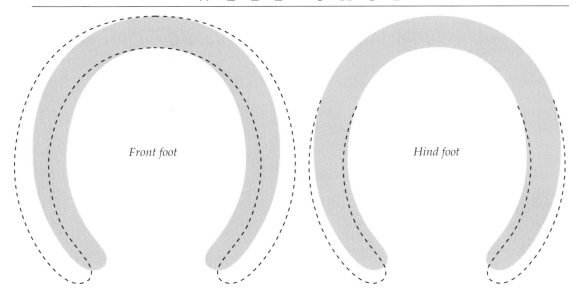

Dotted line indicates shape of manufactured shoes after farrier has worked on them with hammer and anvil.

Front foot

Hind foot

1/ The hammer and anvil in use—opening up the toe of a shoe on the horn of the anvil. This is a shoe for a front foot.

pointed on these shoes. I want to stress that a person needs to *round that toe* on the anvil, even if the shoe looks like it is about the right width. It is important to work the roundness into the toe of the front shoe, and then adjust the branches of the shoe slightly, and maybe turn in the heels a bit. The hind foot is shaped differently from the front foot, so a person might get by without rounding the toe on a hind shoe, and perhaps just straightening the branches. But most hind shoes will need a little rounding, too, for a proper fit.

The reason for rounding the toe is to avoid "quicking" the horse with a nail that is placed inside the white line of the hoof. Nails are meant to go outside the white line, not to the inside of it. A nail that is accidentally driven inside the white line will quick a horse, causing him pain and lameness, and possibly infection in his foot.

By rounding the shoe first, and then adjusting the branches and turning in the heels, you find the nail holes in the shoe are where they need to be in relation to the white line. You can drive your nails in perpendicular to the shoe, with little chance of accidentally quicking the horse.

Here is how to round the toe: Put the shoe over the horn of the anvil and hit the toe three or four times with the rounding hammer, enough to visibly open the shoe.

Next, work on the branches of the shoe by using the horn of the anvil. On a front

2/ *Straightening the branches of the shoe.*

3/ *Turning in the heels of the shoe. Note: These photos were taken on a chilly day. I'm wearing inexpensive cotton roper gloves. They help keep my hands warm, and they are easy to work in.*

shoe, you want a round, symmetrical shoe. On a back shoe, it is usually necessary to straighten the branches a little, but the shoe should remain symmetrical, with one side matching the other. Either rounding or straightening a branch can be done with about three licks with the hammer. For both front and back shoes, hit the shoe so it bends at the first nail hole from the toe. Do this on both sides of the shoe. On a front shoe, go ahead and round the shoe a little more by striking just in front and just behind the row of nail holes. Do this on both sides of the shoe. On a back shoe, strike a few times in the middle region of the nail holes on both sides, and this will

fit the hind foot better.

On both front and back shoes, it is usually necessary to close in the heels slightly. This is the final shoe preparation to be done prior to checking the fit of the shoe before it is nailed on the hoof. After checking the fit, it may be necessary to close the shoe slightly, particularly on a hind foot. Don't overdo it, however. Most beginners try to do entirely too much to the shoe— bend it, close, distort it, mash nail holes shut. These manufactured shoes are pretty

When driving a nail, drive it in easy until you want it to come out of the shell. Then strike hard and the nail will curve out of the shell (or wall) of the hoof.

Pattern

Bevel

Bevel points to outside of hoof.

close to what most horses need. Beginning farriers really get into trouble on fitting shoes because they nearly all want to close a shoe without rounding the toe first. When they do that, it makes the shoe somewhat pointed, the nail holes line up wrong in relation to the white line, and the horse is apt to get quicked with a nail. Even if a shoe looks like it is about the right width, a person still needs to round that toe a little and work the branches around from there for the nail holes to line up where they belong.

Sometimes a horse can get a nail inside the white line and he will not be sore, but there is a good possibility he will end up with a low-grade infection. Then, when the shoe is pulled off and air gets to that infected hole, there is a chance the horse will develop an abscess or at least some soreness.

Nailing

Horseshoe nails are flat-sided, with a pattern on one side only. *Always nail with the pattern facing to the inside of the foot. Always place a nail so it is straight up and down—perpendicular—to the shoe.*

No. 5 city-head nails and No. 5 slim-blade nails are the two main nails we use in shoeing the average saddle horse. A lot of the bigger horses need a No. 6 nail. Very few shoes are punched or fullered to accommodate the regular-head nails, which are good to use in icy country for extra traction, because the heads do not seat in the shoe, but stick out, acting sort of like calks. Most shoes use the city-head, the slim-blade, the counter-sunk, or the platers special. And some of the European shoes are punched to use the E-nail. The E-nail is a European nail with a bigger, boxier head, and a slimmer shank.

Aside from using regular-head nails for

ice, it is important that the nail normally fits easily down in the fullering or the nail hole of the shoe, without being loose or tight. It should just fit, where it goes in, with the press of a finger. If the nail is too tight in the hole, it will cause the shank of the nail to kink through the white line, probably, and make the horse sore. If a nail is just slightly tight in a hole, a shoer can turn the shoe upside-down on the anvil, and back-punch each hole with a pritchel and hammer, to open up the holes enough for a proper fit. But normally, a person can find a wide variety of shoes and nails to fit them at various farrier supply outlets. For horses who have thin shells on their feet, the slim-blade nails are best to use because they are not as apt to split the shells. Horses who are in real dry climates usually have a shell that is thinner and harder and more apt to split than horses who live where it is moist.

Learning to nail properly is one of the hardest things about horseshoeing. The reason: When a person starts to drive a nail, the shoe wants to slide back on the foot.

This tendency to slide back on the foot is caused by the downstroke motion of the hammer.

Here is how to prevent that from happening: Set the shoe on the foot, with the outside tip of the toe on the shoe even with the outside shell on the horse's foot. *Then drive the first heel nail.*

Next, make sure the shoe is still in place, then drive the other heel nail. By starting with the heel nails, you can generally get the shoe stabilized where you can drive the other nails without a problem.

When driving nails, drive them in easy until you want that nail to come out of the shell. The way the nail is made, with the bevel on the end, when you strike harder, it makes the nail curve to the outside, and come out the shell of the foot. The higher you can drive a nail, before making it come out of the shell, the stronger it will be, and the more stable the shoe will be on the foot. The nails should come out about ¾-inch from the bottom of the foot. If you

Shoeing a Front Foot

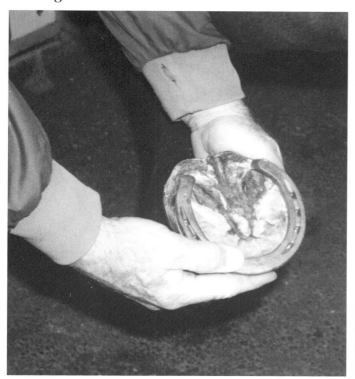

1/ Checking to make sure the shoe fits the foot. The toe of the shoe has been opened, the branches straightened a little, and the heels turned in slightly.

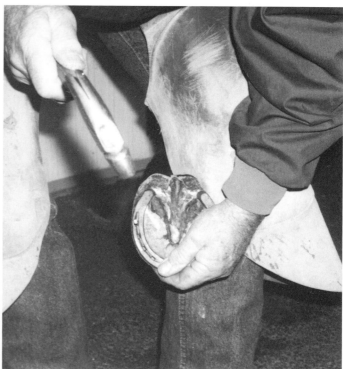

2/ The first nail is driven. This is always a back nail. My left hand holds the shoe in place while the nail is being driven.

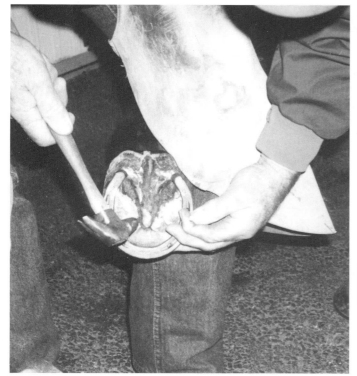

3/ The second nail is driven. This is also a back nail, opposite the first nail driven.

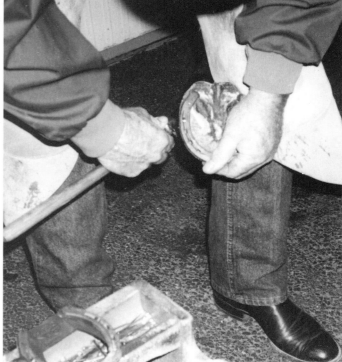

4/ I pause to wring off the sharp end of the first nail, where it is protruding through the hoof wall. I will do the same to the second nail. If the horse continues to stand quietly, I will probably place the remaining four nails, then wring them off after that. If the horse is fidgety, it would be safer to wring each nail off right after it is driven, to lessen the possibility of having the sharp end of a nail jerked into my leg.

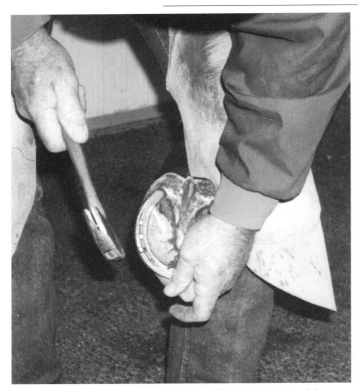

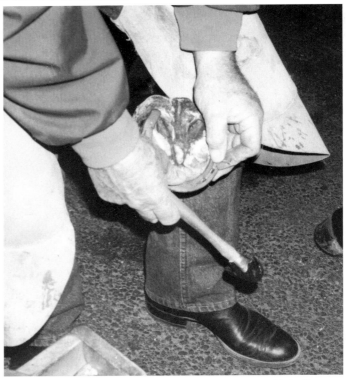

5/ I chose to drive the third and fourth nails on the outside of the shoe. I could also have driven the fourth nail on the inside; it would have made no difference.

6/ The fifth nail is being placed in the second-to-last nail hole (from the heel) in preparation for nailing.

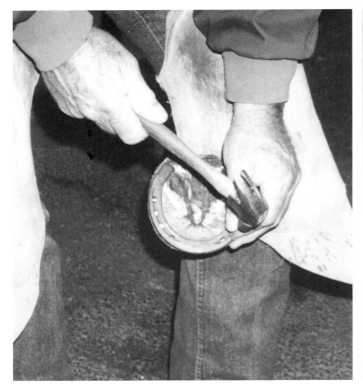

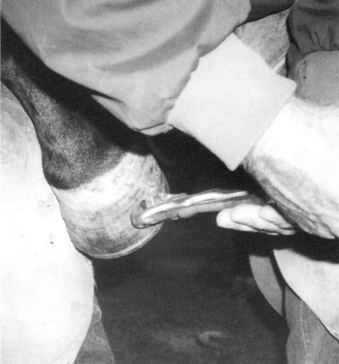

7/ The sixth and last nail is being driven. Note that the two nail holes closest to the toe have not been used.

8/ Using the pull-off tongs to nip off the remaining nails that were poking out on both the inside and outside halves of the hoof.

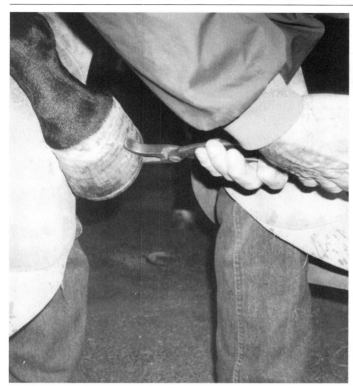

9/ *I have used the fine edge of the rasp to brush against the hoof imme-diately below each nail on this side of the hoof. Now I am clinching down the stubby ends of the nails.*

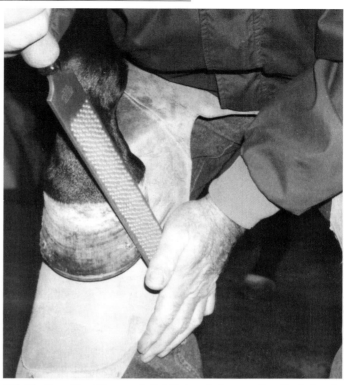

10/ *The fine side of the rasp is lightly brushed across the clinched nails and hoof sides a time or two, smoothing the surface on that side of the hoof.*

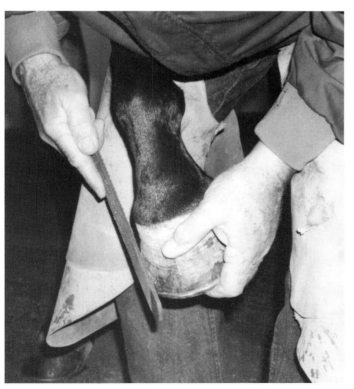

11/ *The same procedures seen in photos 9 and 10 are applied to the other side of the hoof. This shows the fine edge of the rasp brushing against the hoof immediately below each nail. This will be fol-lowed by clinching and then smoothing the sur-face. After this, that same fine edge of the rasp will be floated along the out-side seam between hoof and shoe for the final, smoothing touch. The foot is shod.*

get one nail higher than the others, do not try to clinch it down extra tight to bring it in line with the others. A nail inadvertently driven extra high will not hurt the horse, because the shell of the foot is the same thickness from the bottom of the foot nearly to the top.

Note: If you sense a nail is going in crooked, or you see it start to bend while driving it, stop and pull it out, either with the claw of the hammer or with the pull-off tongs. Start again with a new nail. Do not try to redrive a bent nail, or continue to drive a bent nail after trying to straighten it with your fingers or the hammer. To do that will likely crimp the nail to the inside of the white line.

Nearly all shoes are punched with eight nail holes. But six nails will hold the shoe sufficiently in place when horses will not be climbing through mountains or rocks. The fewer nail holes you can put in a foot, the better. So, which holes do you not nail? For best results, leave the two nail holes alone that are closest to the toe. This leaves three nails on each side of the shoe, not too far forward, not too far back. To put six nails all to the front would create a lack of support on the back half of the shoe. And, nailed in that fashion, if a horse did something to pull a shoe off, it would probably do more damage to the hoof than it would if the shoe had been nailed in the back nail holes.

We just stressed the importance of keeping the shoe from sliding back on the foot during nailing. This is even more critical if all nail holes are used. If a shoe slides back on the foot even a little bit, the two nails up by the toe will be most likely to quick the horse. Even if the two most forward nails are not driven, do not be tempted to let a shoe slide back and continue nailing, with the idea of "dubbing" the toe off with

a rasp so it comes out even with the toe of the shoe. To do that makes that foot shorter in the break-over every step the horse takes. He will be out of balance, especially if the shoe on the opposite foot did not slip back, and he will be in constant stress until the situation is corrected.

Dubbing a toe off like that also weakens the front of that foot, and the heel will begin to contract as the foot grows out to the front. For these reasons, letting a shoe slip back, then dubbing the toe off to make it "look right," is one of the worst mistakes made when shoeing a horse.

I mentioned earlier that I like to shoe a horse with a full heel, in which the heel of the shoe goes back to the bulb of his foot. But nailing on a shoe with a heel that is longer than that is also a mistake, especially if the farrier merely "spins" the heel, or turns or curls it under the horse's foot, rather than take time to cut off the excess length. When a shoe is closed up too much with the heel spun, a horse can pick up a rock. The rock will be held in the crevice of the foot, in the frog and bar area, and the horse's foot cannot shed it the way he should be able to. So going to a little shorter shoe, or cutting the heels off to the ends of the quarter, is a necessity. To curl the heels around puts the foot in stress all the time the horse wears that shoe.

Clinching

It is a good idea to cut off the sharp end of a nail (or wring off the nail with a hammer claw) soon after it has been driven and comes out of the shell. Holding a hoof between your legs with the sharp ends of nails pointing toward you deserves immediate attention. In this situation, a horse could try to pull his foot away and poke your hand or leg with one or more nails. Of course, this is the biggest reason for wearing a leather shoeing apron with extra thicknesses of leather around the knees and thighs.

A shoer can use his pull-off tongs to nip off each nail, or wring off each nail with a hammer, right after it is driven. Then he uses the pull-off tongs or alligator tongs to clinch all the nails down after the last nail is driven on a hoof. If the horse is standing quietly, you might drive your first couple nails, or even all the nails, before nipping off the sharp ends and clinching them. Nipping off or wringing off each nail right after it is driven is the safest for the horseshoer.

There is more than one way to finish a hoof at this point. Most of the time, it is best to take the fine side of the rasp and just barely brush it under each nail on the shell. Then clinch the nails down. This provides a reasonably smooth finish.

Do not "dig a ditch" with the rasp under each nail. These parallel ditches, as I call them, are a common mistake. They let out the natural oil in the horse's foot, and a lot of times may be cut so deeply that they take on moisture that is not needed around the nails. Sometimes while you dig these ditches, the nails can be partially cut through, causing the clinches to break.

On show horses, I generally cut the nails as close as possible to the shell of the hoof. I clinch them down to the point that the hoof is almost completely smooth to the touch, so a person can hardly feel a clinched nail on the hoof. But to finish a nail so finely on a ranch horse would be a mistake. A horse like that needs a little more of the nail left on the outside before it is clinched down, or he will likely lose his shoes to the rocks and rough country in which he lives and works.

Hammer clinching is generally the smoothest and strongest form of clinching. This is where a hammer and clinch block are used. Clinch the nail, and then put the block under the head of the nail, and hammer the clinch to bring it down even tighter against the outside of the hoof. With the hammer clinch, you get a direct bend and very seldom pull any of the shell down on the horse's foot.

By contrast, the alligators have a tendency to roll the clinch, and there is a possibility of opening the nail hole enough to let in some moisture, which will deteriorate the nail. With hammer clinching, there is little chance of moisture getting in.

If you are having trouble with the inside nails on the hind feet, having trouble with the horse stepping on them and pulling them down while he is being used, hammer clinching those inside nails will often solve the problem.

Caution: When hammer clinching, it is important to set the block against each nail, and then hit each nail the same number of times and with the same amount of force. Do not hit one nail six times and another nail three times. You do not want to concentrate this tightness in one or two nails—it needs to be spread evenly among all the nails. Hit each nail maybe twice.

The final touch is to take the fine edge of the rasp and draw it around the edge of the shoe, brushing the outside of the shell where it comes in contact with the shoe, putting in a tiny groove all the way around the shoe. This is called fitting a sand crack. It keeps the shoe from putting excessive stress on the bottom of that outside shell, it gives a real finished appearance to the hoof, and it takes away any sharpness, to make sure no one cuts a hand when picking up the foot to clean it.

Resetting Shoes?

I do not do much resetting, even if the shoes do not show a lot of wear after they have been pulled. Even with a little wear—on the toe, to the inside, or to the outside of the shoe—putting that shoe back on might cause the horse to start doing some things differently in his feet and legs. Putting on new shoes each time the horse is shod goes a long way toward keeping him lined up and moving properly.

A reset shoe will likely have a sharp edge to it, and if that horse should overreach and bump a front leg, he could do

Shoeing a Hind Foot

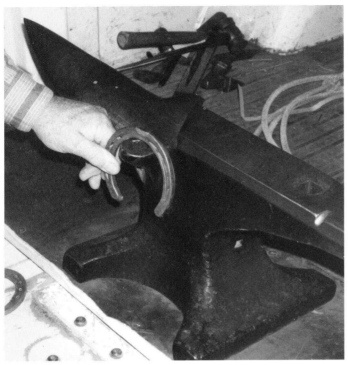

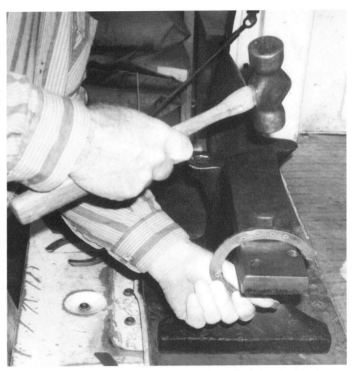

1/ I square the toes on hind shoes quite often—especially for horses who have a tendency to forge. And I do this almost routinely on rope horses, or any performance horse who is asked for sudden bursts of speed. This squaring lessens the chance of the horse striking a front foot or leg while moving at speed. I am starting to square the toe on this shoe for a hind foot by placing the toe of the shoe over the turning ring on the anvil, and striking the toe with the hammer.

2/ Next, I straighten the branches of the shoe a little by placing the shoe over the heel of the anvil in this fashion and striking several times with the hammer.

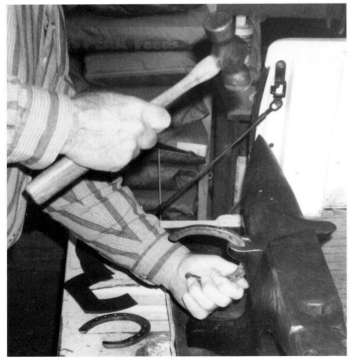

3/ Using the turning ring to help work a little more squareness in both sides of the toe.

4/ I am picking up the shoe after having laid it flat on top of the anvil and checking to see that the shoe has remained level after altering it. A shoe that does not sit level on the anvil can be tapped with the hammer until it is flush with the anvil.

5/ The horse I am shoeing also has a stifle problem, and the veterinarian has recommended she be shod with a moderate wedge pad on both hind feet. This is a manufactured partial wedge pad that I like to use.

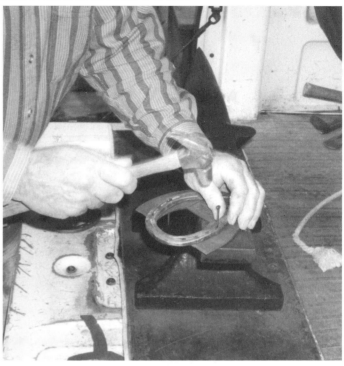

6/ I "tack" the pad to the shoe by placing a nail in the last hole on both sides of the shoe.

7/ The nails are then wrung off.

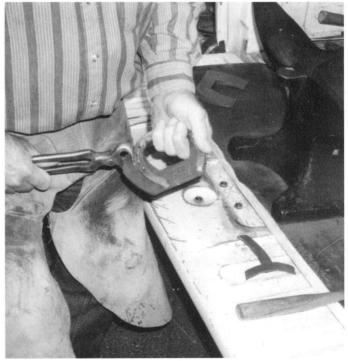

8/ I use nippers to nip away the excess material around the outside of the shoe.

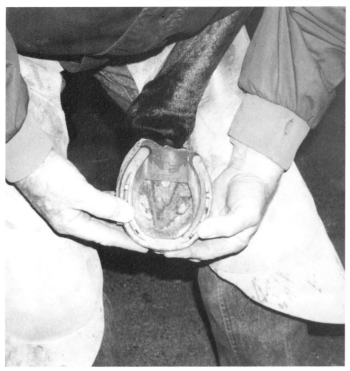

9/ Placing the shoe on the back foot. The fit is correct. Note the squareness in the toe.

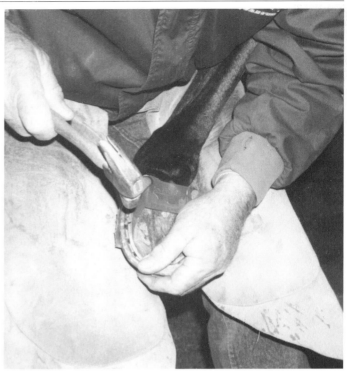

10/ I begin by nailing the second-to-last hole on one side of this shoe. If the wedge pad was not being used, I would start in the last holes, closest to the heels.

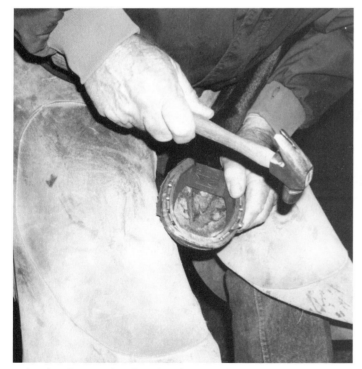

11/ I placed a second nail on the other side of the shoe in the second hole from the toe. I could have put it one more hole down from the toe, and it would have worked just as well there. However, there was a thinner portion of pad under this nail hole, and therefore it was easier and quicker for me to place my second nail there. At this point, there are two nails holding the shoe on the foot.

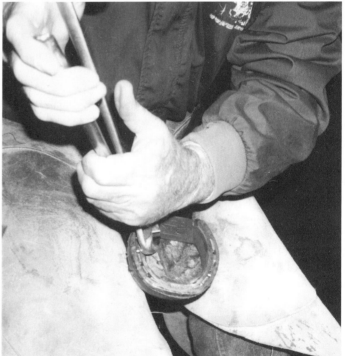

12/ Using crease-pullers or pull-off tongs, I can then remove the two nails that were originally holding the pad to the shoe.

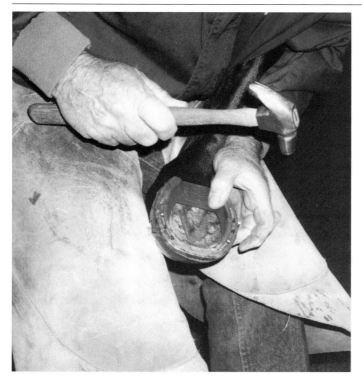

13/ I can now place nails in the two holes closest to the heel, and then put in the sixth and last nail. I will dress the hoof off with rasp and clincher the same way I did it on the front foot.

I like to use different types of shoes on horses during the course of a year, because of the difference in length and positioning of nail holes.

more damage to himself than with a new, blunt shoe. Also, the nail holes of a used shoe will have to be cleaned out before it can be put back on, and the shoe will still probably have to be straightened on the anvil. A horse might even need a different size shoe than he did the last time. A stretch of dry weather versus a stretch of wet weather can sometimes change a horse's foot one full size. Wet weather expands hoofs.

The Change-Up

I like to use different types of shoes on horses during the course of a year, because of the difference in length and positioning of nail holes. I do not suggest anyone go overboard in wanting to do different things to a horse every time he is shod, but subtle changes from time to time can promote a healthy hoof.

Sometimes I take shoes and cut them off and change their length and shoe a horse with a slight difference in the heel. Or I may take a bigger shoe and cut it down to fit a smaller horse. This changes the nailing in the foot, and that alone helps to keep a hoof healthy.

Breed Variations

Morgans and Arabians are probably the soundest horses of any. Very seldom do we find one of them with things like sidebone or ring-bone. They both have a little different set in their ankles and joints, and this seems to give them more elasticity in their legs. Morgans and Arabians seem to wear their shoes more evenly than other breeds. Just an observation.

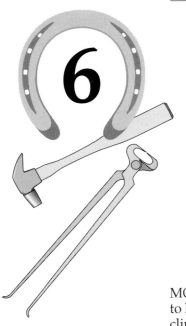

THE FORGE

MOST OF THE forge work a person needs to learn these days involves pulling side clips or toe clips, turning heel calks, jumping a weld on a bar shoe, welding a corner on a shoe, or welding a heel calk down. Portable gas forges and coal forges are available at most farrier supply outlets. Personally, I prefer a coal forge, for these reasons.

The gas heats a shoe more slowly than a

coal forge, and I think there is a tendency to leave a shoe in the gas forge longer for that reason. If a shoe is left in the fire too long, it gets too hot and begins to flake off. The result is a thinner shoe. A coal forge is hotter, quicker, and a person therefore learns to work more quickly. Also, you can heat the area you want a little easier with a coal forge, without heating the whole shoe.

On the other hand, gas forges are much cleaner than coal. A gas forge can also be used on a cold day to take the chill off the area I will be working in (one can warm his hands over a coal forge, but it probably will not take the chill off the rest of the area). The soft coal necessary for a forge is also more of a problem to obtain, but there are still sources around the country where you can get it. Most of the good coal I get comes from Oklahoma, and a lot of good coal comes out of Kentucky and Pennsylvania. This is all generally a soft coal, which maintains a good, clean heat, and most of it does not have much sulphur content. The hard coals seem to burn down and get metal too hot, and there is also a problem with clinker buildup on hard coal.

A coal forge will get hot enough to make a good, clean weld. With a gas forge, it takes more time to get enough heat to weld, and a person definitely needs to use a flux or ether braze with the gas forge.

Caution

In the days of the old blacksmith shops, where folks brought their horses to be shod,

(Continued on page 84)

This is the small coal forge I originally created back in 1962. It is made of light sheet metal rolled into a cone. It will burn a cup of coal at a time, and one cup will usually do four shoes, depending on the work being done. The forge blower came from an old car heater. It blows air into the forge, making for a quick, hot fire. To operate the blower, one wire is connected to an electrical source (like a 12-volt battery), and the other is simply a ground wire that connects from the blower to a piece of metal.

To start the forge fire, I open the door and remove any clinkers (from the last fire) from the bottom. The bottom of the forge, which holds the fire, is called the "duck's nest." I wad up a couple sheets of newspaper, light it, put on a cup of coal, and then turn on the air. After about 3 minutes, the fire goes out and the coals are left, glowing red.

I can put in up to four shoes at a time. For example, I may slip in (using the fire tongs) four shoes with the left branches resting in the fire. After about a minute, I will turn the shoes so the right branches are in the fire. I will then turn off the air and begin doing whatever I need to do on the shoes—trimming heels off, rolling toes, pulling clips, whatever. The air blowing on the coal is what creates the most intense heat, so I will not have that high degree of heat on the shoes that are simply resting in the forge, waiting to be worked.

A shoe is ready to be worked when it starts to glow red.

To weld something on a shoe requires even more heat. Metal is hot enough to weld together—which means fusing it together by striking with the rounding hammer—when it glows a bright orange in the forge, then turns white and sparks begin to fly off it. This tells you the metal is at the melting point.

Remember, a shoe should not be quenched in the water until it has turned gray. Remember, too, to use fire tongs when handling hot shoes—a gray-colored shoe might not appear to be hot, but it is!

A lot of farriers operate their portable forges from the back of their pickup beds. This works well for me too. But to lessen fire danger, a person might want to set up the forge away from the pickup and anything else that might potentially catch fire.

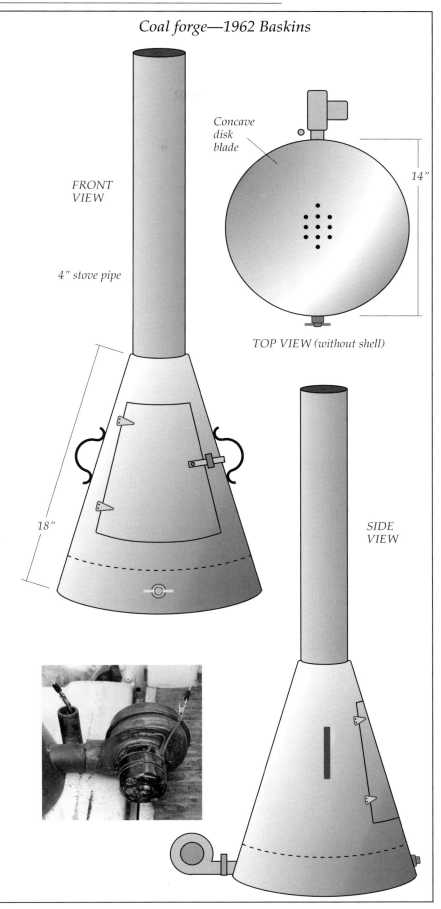

Coal forge—1962 Baskins

Concave disk blade

14"

TOP VIEW (without shell)

FRONT VIEW

4" stove pipe

18"

SIDE VIEW

After a farrier has shod horses for a few years, and has his practice established, he can do a lot of his forge work at home before he goes out to do a week's work.

a lot of forge work was done every day, and there was virtually no fire hazard because the shops were built with safety in mind. But now, with the farrier going to different places with his portable forge, there can be a lot of potentially dangerous things sitting around, like gasoline, kerosene, and diesel, and of course hay or parched grass and weeds. So, it pays to remember to exercise caution when using a fire.

After a farrier has shod horses for a few years, and has his practice established, he can do a lot of his forge work at home before he goes out to do a week's work. This procedure works well for a person who has in mind all the places he will be going and the horses who need to be shod. A guy can still carry the forge, but not have to set it up all the time.

A lot of horses who have real shelly, bad feet, will still need to have a fire, to seat hot shoes on their feet. The heat draws the natural oil in the hoof to the surface and makes for a hard seat on a shoe. But as a rule, one can do about as much good with a cold shoe.

For example, by using the concave roller-motion shoe (see the chapter on corrective trimming and shoeing) on a horse like this, there can be enough stress placed on the outside shell to keep this type of foot growing and doing what it needs to do.

There are some other considerations to keep in mind, when using hot shoes on a horse. Some shoers get in a hurry, and quench a hot shoe when it is still *too* hot, so practice should correct this tendency. With a drop-forged shoe, if you cool it when it is still red-hot as you put it in the water, that shoe will get so hard it becomes brittle. If you need to make a minor adjustment on it with hammer and anvil, the shoe is apt to break.

If a shoe like this is left on a horse a long time and the horse wears it out, there is a good chance the shoe will split in the toe

and break. When it does, it will open up, and often half the shoe will come off the foot, and the other half will stay on. The part that comes off will often take a lot of the hoof with it.

Note: When a shoe is quenched in water, it will shrink slightly, so it is very important when a shoer goes to nail the shoe on, that the size is re-checked. The shrinkage may have made the shoe too narrow to fit the foot properly. As a rule, a shoer can put the shoe over the horn of the anvil, open it one good whack with the hammer, and it will open the shoe back to where it was when first fit to the foot. If this is not done, the shoe will probably not fit the seat that was burned into the foot ahead of time.

Maintaining a uniform hardness in a shoe is important. Getting horses to use their feet similarly to each other is the important thing, and should be watched. The next time I shoe a horse, I can observe how the shoes are worn, and if the shoes are worn pretty much equally, then I know I am on the right track with that horse, whether he was shod hot or cold. If part of a hot shoe is harder than another part— because of too much heat and/or too-rapid cooling, this can cause a problem with how that shoe wears.

For example, if a shoer is cutting the branches on a hot shoe, and heating, cutting, and cooling the shoe to do one branch, then heating, cutting, and cooling the shoe to do the other branch, the result will be one branch that was heated and cooled differently from the other. That will mean half the shoe is harder than the other, and will therefore wear differently. If a shoe does not wear as much on one side as the other, that horse will be out of balance in a matter of 10 days to 2 or 3 weeks, and this will cause him some discomfort in the way he is moving. It does not seem like a fraction of an inch of wear would make any difference, but it really does. Remember in the chapter on trimming, when I explained how a couple cuts of the rasp can change the whole way a horse moves? The same principle applies here.

When working the shoes hot, I put

Pulling a Toe Clip

1/ A person who learns to pull a good clip on a shoe can do anything else he wants in the way of making or altering shoes by means of forge and anvil. This is one of two front shoes I placed in the forge, toe first, to heat. While I was heating both shoes, I turned them over once, to help with even heating. When the shoes started glowing red in the toe areas, I shut off the air (which creates the intense heat) and removed one shoe to start working on pulling a toe clip. The shoe is seated over the clip horn on the anvil. This photo shows the clip beginning to form after only one strike with the rounding hammer.

2/ After four or five strikes with the hammer, the clip is really beginning to take shape.

3/ *I finish drawing the clip. The hammer strikes are down and toward me.*

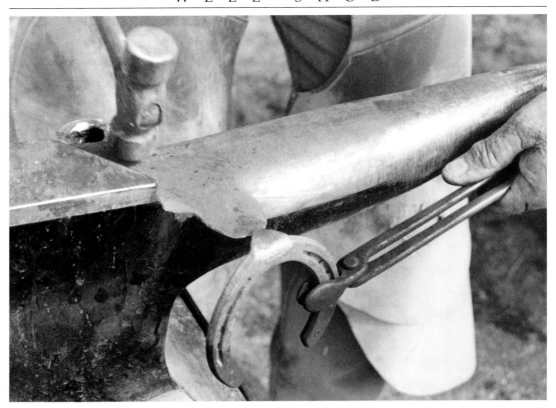

4/ *Squaring the clip back to the shoe.*

5/ The shoe should be level on the anvil, and the clip should be at 90 degrees to the rest of the shoe, at this point.

6/ The clip is hammered beyond the 90-degree angle, to conform with the angle of the horse's hoof.

7/ *Viewing the clip, checking to see that the downward angle of the clip has not resulted in any distortion or twisting of the clip.*

8/ *Leveling the shoe again. Working on the clip created a slight distortion in the rest of the shoe.*

9/ The shoe has just been fitted to the horse's hoof, while it was still hot, then removed and quenched in the water bucket.

10/ A few strokes of the rasp will put a smooth finish on the clip.

11/ A close look at the finished shoe with toe clip. The same procedure will now be used on the second shoe. Then both shoes can be nailed on.

either two or four shoes in the fire at a time, starting with one branch of each shoe facing into the fire. With four shoes, I typically trim a front foot and back foot, go to the fire and remove one shoe, cut off one branch, replace the shoe—turning it over in the fire to heat the other branch—and do this to the other three shoes, as well.

Then I go back to the horse, trim the other front foot and the other hind foot, return to the fire and cut off the other branch from each shoe. After that, I put the toes of the shoes in the fire, to make any adjustments to them, like squared toes or round toes. After this, I proceed to burn each shoe on the respective hoofs, using the tongs to hold a shoe, one at a time. And it is only after this that I put the shoes in the water to cool them, one at a time, after burning each shoe on each hoof. Each shoe will have cooled enough before going into the water to where it will have the same hardness overall. And uniform hardness is what we want, generally speaking.

Uniform hardness is what we want in a shoe, generally.

Calks and Blocks

There are times, however, when it is desirable to have part of a shoe harder, and therefore more resistant to wear, than the rest of the shoe. Turning heel calks on a hot shoe, or building a block heel on a shoe are such examples in which I want extra durability in the heel area, and therefore want the shoe to be harder in that area. By getting both heels of a shoe red-hot in the fire, then quenching just that portion of the shoe, the heels will take a lot more wear than the rest of the shoe. By hammering this metal, making the block heel and shaping and fitting it all, we work-harden it, as well. Then quenching it in the water makes it extra hard. Actually, calks are used on very few

horses these days. With some jumping horses and a few cutting horses who have a problem sliding through too far and not getting stopped for a turn, I use calks on them. I use grass calks on some rodeo horses who are used in grass, rather than dirt, arenas.

Side Clips

When using side clips, get the clips hot and seat the shoe on the foot. That will burn the edge of the foot so the side clip can seat perfectly on the foot. Then the clip can be hammered down and have a real smooth fit. To learn how to pull the side clip, save your old shoes and then run them through the fire, get them hot and learn how to pull a nice clip. It is something that just takes practice, and yet few people really learn how to pull a nice clip. A clip should be pulled and be in the area of $3/4$ of an inch tall and $3/4$ of an inch wide. This takes a pretty good piece of steel out of the shoe, so it does take practice, but practice makes perfect.

I use a side clip if a horse has a quarter-crack or an old scar. I put the clip in front of the scar or behind the scar or quarter-crack, whichever holds the foot together the best.

Toe Clips

To "jump" a toe clip requires a coal fire, as most gas forges do not get hot enough to do the necessary welding. To begin, I pull a small clip from the toe of the shoe, and then forge-weld a larger clip on top of that. This takes a lot of practice too. The only way to learn it is to practice on old shoes.

I use a toe clip mainly on a big horse who is used for jumping, or a horse who has a real thin shell. In both cases, a toe clip helps keep the shoe in place—it creates an extra hold. But very few horses need a toe clip if the farrier can drive a good high nail.

Creating an Egg Bar Shoe
From a Manufactured Shoe

1/ I started with shoes that were two sizes larger than what the horse would normally wear. This gave me enough extra length in the heels of the shoes to create the bars. The heels of the shoes were heated evenly, until they were glowing red in the forge. This shoe was removed and I am working on drawing out (lengthening) one of the heels by striking it with the rounding hammer. The hammer strokes are downward and outward, away from me.

2/ I use both the heel and horn of the anvil to draw the heels of the shoe.

3/ Now I am tapering the heels with the hammer.

4/ The heels are being turned in to one another.

5/ The bottom (or heel) of the hammer handle is used to clean the areas where the weld will be made, knocking away any slag and scale from the shoe. This also burns the hickory handle just a little, and the slight smear of ash left on the shoe acts as a flux, which enhances the weld.

6/ Bringing the tapered heels together in preparation for welding.

7/ Closing the heels.

8/ The heels are closed, and the shoe is now ready to go back in the fire, where it will be heated in this area—white-hot—to make the weld. In my forge, it takes a couple minutes of heating to reach this temperature. While this is going on, I work on the second shoe.

9/ The shoe is removed and the two heels are welded together by striking several times with the rounding hammer.

10/ The shoe is placed over the horn of the anvil and struck in this fashion to help maintain the roundness to the area.

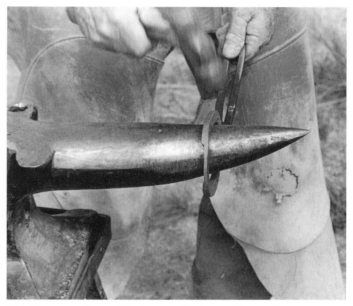

11/ The heel was heated again to white-hot, then placed over the edge of the anvil like this and struck several times to recess the bar area. Note that the bottom of the shoe is facing downward on the anvil.

12/ More rounding out the bar over the horn of the anvil.

13/ *At this point, the bar is held over the angled ledge I have on my anvil and struck several times till it bends slightly. The bend will be upward, when the shoe is on the horse, so it fits over the bulbs of the horse's heel.*

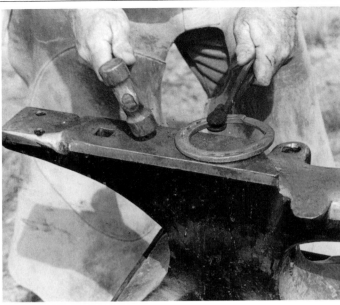

14/ *Leveling the shoe.*

15/ *Concaving the inside of the shoe slightly, to help relieve sole pressure on the horse's foot, and put more stress on the hoof wall.*

16/ *The finished egg bar shoe (or egg-shaped bar shoe). The purpose of a shoe like this is to either apply pressure or relieve pressure in a specific part of the hoof. A bar shoe can do both of these jobs, depending on how it is built and shaped. For example, I want to apply pressure to the hoof wall when shoeing a horse for contracted heels, and I want to alleviate pressure on the heel when shoeing a horse with a quarter crack.*

Trailers

Outside trailers on the hind shoes are really easy to turn. The outside heel is turned outward, and generally the inside heel is cut off so the shoe is not distorted—the trailer comes out in proportion to the rest of the shoe. This is done to give a horse lateral support. When he buries his foot to stop, he stops on his outside heel, and the trailer guides him straight ahead and doesn't let him splay out.

Sliders

It is good to use a fire when putting on slide plates for reining horses or some working cow horses. Most slide plates on the hind feet are so wide, a fire is needed to roll the outside toe or to tip the toe, whatever might need to be done. Also, burning the slide plate on will make it seat better, to where the horse can probably wear it from 4 to 8 weeks. It is important to not get slide plates too hard. If quenched when red-hot, the wide plates will be too hard, and therefore wind up being too slick. The result is the horse will likely slip while running his figure eights in a pattern.

Generally, with slide plates, I roll the outside toe, starting at the center of the toe on the shoe. By rolling in this manner, it makes the shoe hang in the ground a little longer, peeling the dirt away during a slide. And with most slide plates, a horse needs to be lowered on the outside of the foot and have an outside trailer pulled, because the horse stops on the outside heel, and the trailer on this shoe will carry him through a slide and keep him headed straight.

Rasping the nail heads off the slide plates is also important. I generally drive a number $4\frac{1}{2}$ nail on a plate, and that means there is not as much of the head to rasp off. Most of the commercially made plates come with just three holes, but it is good to punch in a fourth hole in the outside of the shoe, because a horse stops on the outside, creating more stress in that area. You can touch a slide plate after a horse has made a

sliding stop, and that shoe will be so hot you can not hold your hand on it. So, that tells us the horse is taking quite a bit of stress on both hind legs by doing these stops.

And note: With young horses, it is good to start them in two or three varieties of slide plates. I start with maybe a saddle horse shoe that is a little longer than normal. After the horse is broke better, has started to stop, and is not afraid of stopping, then I will go to a $\frac{3}{4}$-inch slider and use that on him for one shoeing. Then progress to a 1-inch or $1\frac{1}{4}$-inch tapered shoe. The whole idea is to not scare young horses when they are getting acquainted with the sliding stop. If a horse gets down and maybe tips over backwards during a stop, he will have a real problem getting over an experience like that.

One thing to watch for when hot shoeing—the smoke that comes off will sometimes scare the horse, so it is wise to watch when the hot shoe is first touched to the hoof and smoke begins boiling off of it. But after the horse gets used to the smoke, he will probably not move at all. And if any burn-cutting needs to be done to the hoof, to help a problem (this comes up in corrective trimming and shoeing), I find that after the initial smoke, the horse stands still and relaxes, as if the heat feels good to him. If it gets too hot, the horse will take his foot away. He will not let the farrier do anything too severe to him.

Branding

A farrier with a forge is also called upon to do some branding, particularly horse branding, from time to time. With a coal forge, the irons can be heated to a cherry red, then burned momentarily on a piece of board before being used to brand the

Smoke that comes off will sometimes scare the horse, so it is wise to watch when the hot shoe is first touched to the hoof and smoke begins boiling off of it.

Turning a Heel Calk

1/ Follow these steps involved with turning a heel calk.

2/ The heel has now been folded back on itself, to form the calk.

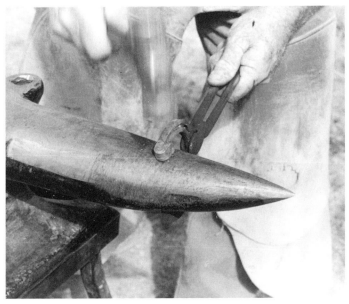

3/ Use the rounding hammer to tap the side and . . .

4/ . . . the end of the calk.

5/ *The heel cutter is used with the cutting hammer to remove the tip-end of the calk, thus making a nice, smooth finish to the heel of the shoe.*

6/ *Finishing up with a few strokes of the rasp.*

7/ *Now, here's how to make an outside trailer on the other heel. This would be done (just on the outside heel) to give a horse lateral support—if he had a tendency to splay out with his back feet during a hard stop. The heel is placed over the horn of the anvil and drawn out with the rounding hammer.*

8/ *The trailer is taking shape. A few hammer strikes on the top of the shoe keeps everything level.*

E L L - S H O D

9/ *The tip of the heel is cut off for a smooth finish.*

10/ *More drawing out of the heel.*

An outside trailer can be used on a variety of shoes, but basically it gives a horse lateral support when he stops.

11/ *The finished trailer (right) with the finished calk. I use this vertical trailer on any horse—pleasure, ranch, trail horse, etc.—who has low heels and tends to get his back feet too far under himself, particularly when he stops.*

98

horse. Generally, there isn't an excessive burn with this method. Placing the iron on the wood initially cleans the iron and eliminates whatever gases accumulated around the red-hot iron during heating. With a gas forge, there is a little more buildup of gas, and even when using the board to clean the iron, there is still a slight tendency for a flame-up during branding, which can blotch the brand. A hot iron should be applied to the animal for about 3 seconds.

Freeze branding is also gaining in popularity. Most of it is done with irons placed in liquid nitrogen, then applied for about 20 seconds (and it can be a trick to keep a horse still for 20 seconds). When freeze branding started to get popular several years ago, it was thought that only stainless steel, copper, or brass irons could be used for it. But I have helped brand several horses with this method, and found that the regular 1/4-inch round iron worked very well.

I have branded horses since I developed the Short Rope Act, and found that I can put the rope above the horse's knee and have the horse tied to a wall, then get his attention—have him look at me. I can then reach ahead to his shoulder, or back to his hip, or wherever the brand is to go, and use clippers on the area to be branded.

After that, when it is time to apply the iron, I can put some stress on the leg with the rope on it—enough stress to make the horse stand on three legs—then apply the brand. And the horse will remain still, resulting in a nice brand. One handy hint for branding horses is to take a piece of board (a 2 by 4 or 1 by 6) that is just a little longer than the branding iron, and use this to steady the iron while the brand is being applied. One end of the board goes against my chest or stomach, and the other end of it goes against the horse, just below where the brand is to be placed. The iron is then run down the board, against the hide. By pushing the board into the horse's shoulder or hip or wherever, the area to be branded is pushed up and stretched slightly, and this also helps make the brand very neat and square.

Branding has nothing to do with taking care of a horse's feet, but it is something that competent farriers are called on to do, and it is all part of the horseshoeing trade. There is no fixed charge for doing any of this, but as a rule, people will often tip a farrier for this service, or buy him a steak.

Sometimes, I am asked to make a branding iron for someone, and I have found that 1/4-inch round steel is best for making an iron for a horse brand. By using round stock, the hair will form a part, and the brand can be easily read even with a long haircoat.

7

CORRECTIVE SHOEING

CORRECTIVE SHOEING involves the alteration of the basic horseshoe, and possibly the combined use of various other materials, to help the horse overcome whatever problem he might have traveling on his own feet. Some altered shoes are also used to help prevent problems or enhance performance. For example, calks or borium on shoes may be needed to help prevent slipping on potentially slick surfaces, like turf, ice, rocks, or pavement. Still, altered shoeing can have its own side effects, as we will see, so a measure of caution should be used when deviating from the simple, basic shoeing job, for reasons other than therapeutic.

Survey of Materials

Generally speaking, a flat shoe is the best for the all-around shoeing job. The only reason to go with any of these other things, that are not therapeutic, is when you are going to a grass arena, or the mountains, or somehow plan on using the horse for something that is out of the ordinary for him. The more natural we can keep a horse's feet, the better. And with a conventional shoe and with a degree of caution, one generally does not need to use borium or studs.

Half-Round Shoe

The half-round shoe—a manufactured shoe—makes the most natural rim on a horse's foot. This shoe comes in ³⁄₈ths, ¹⁄₂, ⁵⁄₈ths, and ³⁄₄ths. The ³⁄₄ths-inch width is too heavy for the average saddle horse, but the lighter shoes are real good to help the horse move in his most natural way. This type of shoe has a natural break-over. There is not a lot of traction with this shoe, so it is not very successful for arena horses that do a lot of running and stopping. But for the horse that is just ridden out on the trail most of the time, this is a good shoe.

The half-round shoe is also pretty good

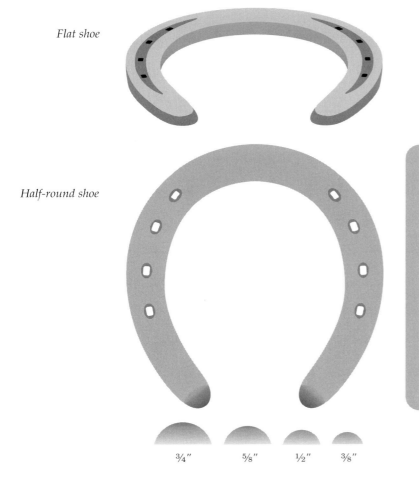

Flat shoe

Half-round shoe

³⁄₄"   ⁵⁄₈"   ¹⁄₂"   ³⁄₈"

to use on horses who have a tendency to be stiff or want to stumble a little, or seem to be using their knees excessively. I also use this shoe frequently on a young horse who is starting into training. Because the edge of the shoe is under the horse's foot, it helps prevent him from reaching across and maybe knocking a splint on the other front leg.

With the half-round, a few of the shoes are made with fullering, but most of them are just counter-sunk, and therefore can be slick. I never use the half-round shoes on the hind feet, unless I use full wedge pads along with them. And this is mainly for trotters and pacers, where we are trying to keep these horses "off themselves."

The heavier or wider half-round shoes will give the horse more motion—more like a gaited horse—and these work for a horse who needs to extend himself more. The lighter half-rounds will make that horse move as near to natural as any shoe to be found. However, some horses will start winging or paddling more in the half-round. The reason for this is because of the roundness of the shoe—the horse can roll his foot any way he wants to, and that is why some horses start winging or paddling in front.

The half-round shoe in the snow will clean out, thus preventing the buildup of snowballs in the feet, but there is no traction in the snow with this shoe. This is kind of a good layup shoe to keep a horse in during the winter, when he is not being used much, but is not going barefooted.

Weighted Shoes

The side-weight shoe is generally a shoe that has to be hand-made and has a wider web inside or outside, wherever more weight is needed. By drawing the shoe lighter on one branch (with forge and hammer), we come up with the side-weight. The side-weight generally goes across the whole toe, and then has a narrow, and lighter, branch on one side. The flight of the horse's foot will generally follow the side the weight is on, to the inside or outside, whichever is desired in the form of correction to the way he travels. By using the side-weight, one can take out a lot of the winging and

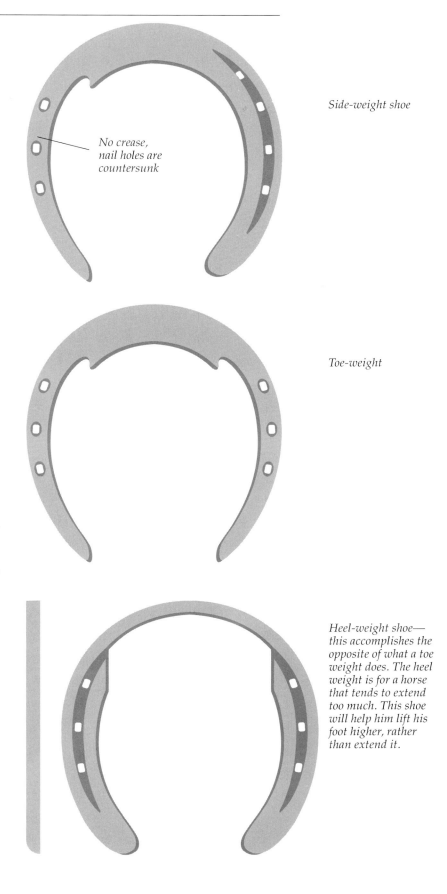

No crease, nail holes are countersunk

Side-weight shoe

Toe-weight

Heel-weight shoe— this accomplishes the opposite of what a toe weight does. The heel weight is for a horse that tends to extend too much. This shoe will help him lift his foot higher, rather than extend it.

paddling and knitting, but this type of shoe should be used only in severe cases.

I use a few toe-weight shoes on some of the Quarter Horses and Thoroughbreds to change motion. For a horse who tends to use too much knee action, a little weight on his toe will make him extend out instead of lifting the leg so high. A toe-weight can be made by drawing a lighter branch on each side of the shoe, back to the heel. I will also roll the toe when I use a toe-weight.

Borium, calks . . .

Horseshoe borium, or the product Stalite, or an excessive calk is really hard on horses' legs because these additions will hang up a horse with each step he takes, so that his foot cannot have any flex to it. Every bit of stress from movement goes right up the joints in the horse's leg. Some of the calks that are forged or screw-in studs are okay, because they can be removed when not needed. But for a horse to be shod and worked full time in borium or calks, it's going to shorten his useful life.

These non-skid materials are mainly for street-parade horses, or for mountain horses, but again, to be able to give horses like these some relief from this excessive traction when it is not needed is very desirable.

Some people think putting borium or Stalite on shoes is a good idea because it will reduce wear on the shoes, make them last longer—and it does! But it also restricts shoes from opening up with the horse's feet as the weeks go by, and this restriction may contribute to problems like ringbone and sidebone.

When calks are used, they should not be turned straight down, but should be tapered to the back or to the front, so there is at least a way for a little slippage to take place as the horse uses his feet. Also, a $\frac{3}{8}$th-inch rise in a calk is about as high as a horse can stand. A $\frac{1}{2}$- or $\frac{3}{4}$-inch high is excessive, and will result in more stress on the foot and ankle than the horse can stand.

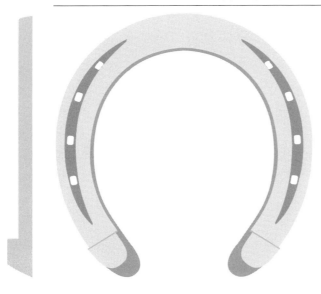

Tapered heel calk

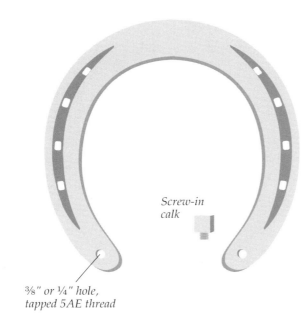

Screw-in calk

⅜" or ¼" hole, tapped 5AE thread

Toe Bar

Another traction device sometimes used on horseshoes is the toe bar. This is a bar across the toe of the shoe, and is used for rocks or rough country. However, the toe bar has a tendency to raise the toe and drop the horse in the heel, and therefore stretches the suspensories in an unnatural way. Generally, a toe bar would be used with a heeled shoe, and as a rule I will put no more than a ¼-inch width of toe bar on a shoe, and then run it nearly across the toe of the foot. With most manufactured shoes, these bars will not be over an inch or 1½-inch long, which is too short. That bar should go nearly clear across the foot, or the horse will tend to break over the inside or outside, and will not travel properly.

Again, some people want to use toed and heeled shoes to get more life out of the shoes, but the trade-off is that there is more stress put on the toe and heel from this type of shoe than from a regular flat shoe. When the toed and heeled shoe is taken off the foot, we will find that it has caused a slight bruise across the toe and heel areas of the foot. This bruising can cause corns and lameness.

Pads

Pads made either of leather or manufactured substance like neoprene are typically used with shoes on horses with a little soreness to their feet. Understand that pads on a horse will often cause that horse to move somewhat differently. He will likely have a different feel of the ground, and either reach higher or use his knee more.

I seldom use pads unless, as I said, a horse seems to need them to help with soreness. Pads used on horses in pastures tend to be a little slick, especially when the pads get wet.

Hand-Made Shoes

A lot of hand-made shoes fashioned out of a wider stock are also real slick out in the grass, so it is not too good to use hand-made or real wide-web shoes on the ranch

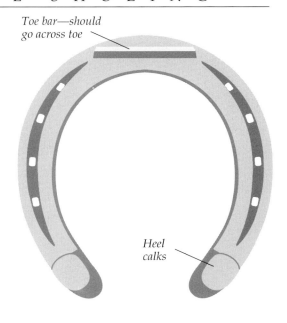

Toe bar—should go across toe

Heel calks

Full pad

Manufactured wedge pads come in 1°, 2°, and 3°, and may be full pads or open. The degree refers to the angle of the pad, from heel to toe, as may be prescribed by a veterinarian.

1° wedge open

Leg Conformation

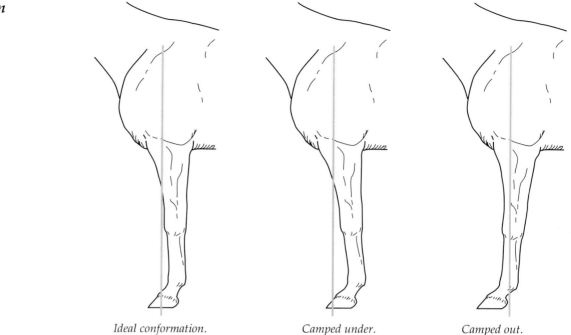

Ideal conformation.   *Camped under.*   *Camped out.*

Knee sprung (buck-kneed).   *Calf-kneed.*

horses working on grass and running and stopping. I do not use wide web shoes a lot. I think their main use is for a horse who had his foot pared out too much, and the foot was too weak to carry a regular shoe.

Evaluating the Horse

Ideally, a horse's owner should be able to evaluate his own horse and be able to tell the horseshoer about any problems that need to be worked on in regards to shoeing. This often is not the case, however, so it is up to the shoer to identify problems and know how to correct them, if possible. A farrier does this by building up his memory bank on all the different problems he has encountered, and what was done to help correct them.

Possible problems observed by noticing the horse's conformation include being toed in, toed out, bowlegged, cow-hocked, camped under, post-legged, buck-kneed, calf-kneed. Closer examination may reveal things like a popped knee, splints, wind puffs, ringbone, contracted heels, cuts around the hoof and ankle areas, seedy toe, bruises, corns, cracks, and thrush.

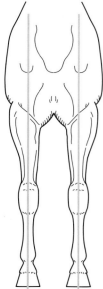

Ideal conformation.

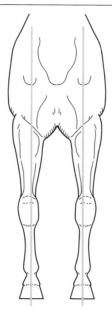

Toes out.

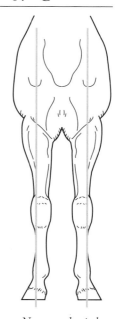

Bowlegged.

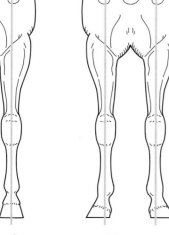

*Narrow-chested
(toes out).*

Good conformation makes shoeing a lot easier. The well-made horse tends to stay sound, no matter what he is used for. Most of the problems the shoer is confronted with in keeping a horse sound stem from one or more of the above conformation faults. There is also a defect I call dropped bulbs, in which the bulbs of the foot are too far behind, and therefore the point of the heel is behind the cannon bone.

With dropped bulbs there is likely going to be trouble with the third phalanx and the navicular bone being dropped down too low and carrying too much stress. For such a horse, we have to cultivate some additional heel growth by shortening the toe on the shoe a little. Most of them need to go in a squared-toe shoe, because they will have a tendency to toe out pretty badly when moving.

A low heel also goes along with a pastern joint that protrudes out above the coronet band. A horse can bump that area and that is what causes most of the bad sidebones. Very seldom does a horse with correct pasterns come up with sidebone or ringbone.

Elongated front feet are another problem which leads to unsoundness with hard work. Horses like this are under constant stress in their feet and are very sus-

Stands close.

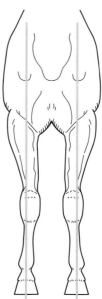

Knock-kneed.

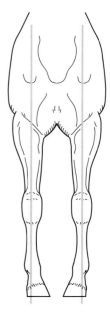

Pigeon-toed.

105

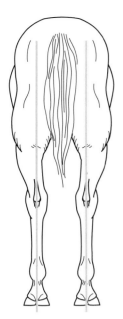

Ideal position.

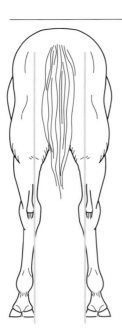

Stands wide.

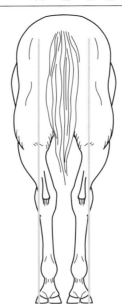

Stands close.

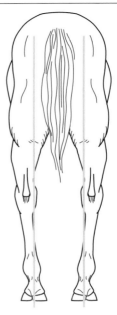

Bowlegged.

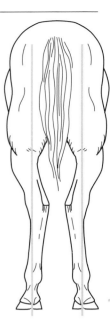

Cow-hocked.

ceptible to founder. This seems to go along with post-leggedness.

Common foot and leg problems that can be detected while watching a horse in motion include things like rope walking, paddling or winging, and varieties of lameness that may turn out to be such things as sore knees, shinbucks, broken bars in the foot, ringbone, navicular disease, and founder. With severe founder in the front feet, a horse will not even want to move, and will stand with hind legs well underneath, attempting to take off pressure from the extremely sore front feet.

An owner can lead a horse around while the farrier watches how he moves, but one of the best means of observation is to put the horse loose in a pen and watch him move at will, or encourage him to move around, if necessary. Watch him walk, trot, canter, stop, turn around.

When watching a horse for signs of soreness, the first place I look is at his ears. The extra movement of his ears will show which foot or leg is really bothering him. If a horse is hurting in the right front, his right ear will dip back each time he puts that foot down.

If his right hind leg is hurting, that same right ear will point down and back each time that foot comes down.

The opposite applies to the left side. His head will also likely bob, slightly to very noticeably, away from the painful side. The horse's tail is another warning flag. The tail will swish noticeably when a problem foot makes contact with the ground as the horse moves around. Of course, one can watch the feet and get an indication of soreness, too. Also, if a horse is sore in both front feet, or both hind feet, he will take short (and maybe halting) steps. If all feet are sore, he will not want to travel at all.

A closer hands-on look may reveal heat and swelling in an area of the leg, ankle, or hoof. Perhaps the horse flinches when the farrier picks up a foot, or refuses to let his foot be picked up—these can all be signs of pain.

At the onset of any lameness that is questionable as to its cause, or questionable as to whether proper or corrective shoeing will provide the sole solution to the problem, a veterinarian should be consulted. The vet may need to do a series of stress tests, nerve blocks, and X-rays to determine the exact cause of the problem, which could be anything from founder, to a cracked coffin

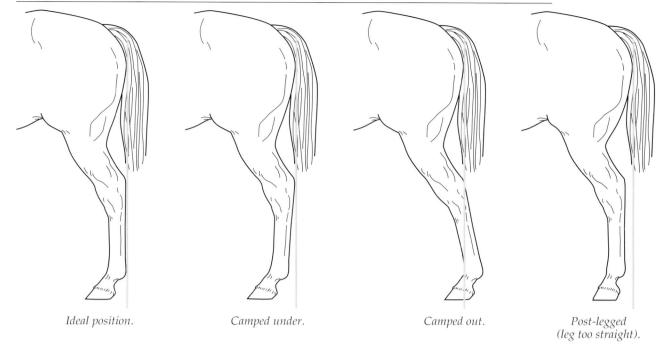

Ideal position.　　　*Camped under.*　　　*Camped out.*　　　*Post-legged
(leg too straight).*

bone, to navicular disease. In most of these instances, a veterinarian and horseshoer can work together to get a horse sound again—or at least as sound as possible. Treatment will often be a combination of internal medicine and corrective shoeing.

The following are all equine foot or leg ailments or imperfections that the farrier is likely to encounter as he makes his shoeing rounds. They range from minor blemishes to severe lamenesses. Many can be helped with the proper kind of shoes and shoeing.

Broken Bars

I believe there are more horses that go lame from fracturing a bar in the bottom of a foot than just about anything else. Sometimes an owner will mistake a broken bar for navicular disease. Hoof testers can be used on such a foot, and results similar to navicular disease will show up. In other words, the foot is sore. The break in a bar can be seen only if the hoof is thoroughly cleaned out prior to examination. A farrier who can discover a broken bar on a lame horse like this can cure the problem and save the owner a trip to the veterinarian.

The bars support the entire foot, and if one of them is broken—the result of injury,

stepping hard on a hard object—then the horse will likely show signs of lameness when turning to the right or left, whichever side the break is on. Horses who are shod or trimmed regularly seldom have trouble with a broken bar. This problem happens usually to horses who are allowed to grow real long feet. The horse may pick up a rock that gets wedged in his foot, and the bar breaks as he walks on it.

Generally, we can pare down this foot and use a shoe that is a little wider than normal, to give the foot a bit more support, and in a matter of three or four days, the horse should be reasonably sound.

If a horse breaks a bar in his back foot, he will act like he has a stifle problem, so this is another area of diagnosis that needs to be done carefully. For a broken bar in a back foot, we can put this horse in a squared-toe shoe, and set it back off of his toe about $3/8$ths to $1/2$ inch. This will tie that foot together and make this horse much more sound than simply shoeing his back feet normally.

Leg Problems

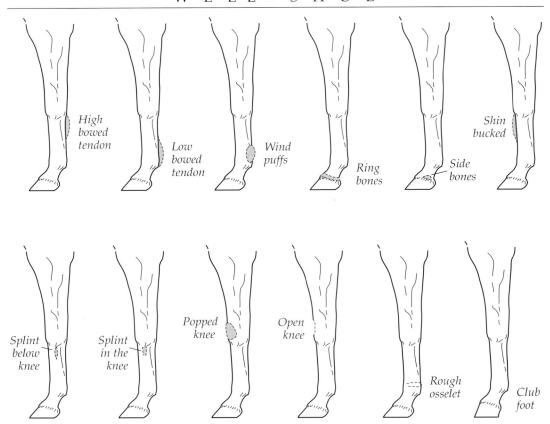

Bow-Legged

The bow-legged horse is quite common. This horse is too wide in his hocks. A lot of times this horse will also tend to roll his ankles over, as well. Such hocks also tend to be a little weak. Bow-legged horses need the inside of their feet trimmed lower, and then a squared-toe shoe, which will help the foot break over more correctly, and will help keep the horse from getting sore.

The bow-legged horse is also prone to having bad frogs on his feet, and "jacks" (bone spavin) on his hind legs. The calked ankle shoe (#3) with calk to the outside can be used on the bow-legged horse, along with a squared toe. The single calk on the outside will help prevent the severely bow-legged horse from twisting his foot into the ground with each step. Bow-legged horses may also develop wind-puffs, and if a horse is developing these, squaring the toe on those hind shoes, and leaving the shoes long enough to offer additional lateral support, will help prevent the continuation of this problem. Such a horse will likely be pigeon-toed on those hind feet.

The main thing we want to accomplish on a bow-legged horse is to stabilize his hocks, so the hocks do not roll out to the side with every step the horse takes. If a foot is level or high on the inside, this will cause the hock to roll and flex with every step, and the result, sooner or later, will be the creation of a bog spavin or blood spavin, resulting in soreness. By leaving the outside of the foot high on most of these horses, the foot will point straight ahead when dropped like a pendulum, and not toe in or toe out. This will possibly lessen the distance between hocks by 3 or 4 inches.

A horse who is bow-legged behind will usually be straight in front. Conversely, if a horse has a conformation problem with his front legs, he will often have good conformation with his hind legs.

Bowed Tendon

A bowed tendon is the result of injury to the tendon along the backside of one or

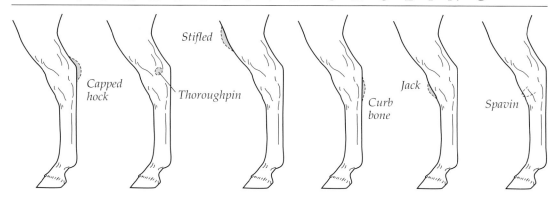

Capped hock

Stifled

Thoroughpin

Curb bone

Jack

Spavin

both front legs. Often, this occurs in race horses (usually high up on the leg), or rope horses (usually lower on the leg), or on jumpers. Typically, it occurs when the horse is being stressed, working at speed; probably when the leg is fully extended to the rear and that tendon gets struck with a hind foot over-reaching, or maybe gets struck from another horse running next to him. Seldom do we see ranch horses, pleasure horses—or even barrel horses—with bowed tendons. In the case of barrel horses, they are usually shod with conventional shoes, not racing plates, which lessens the stress on their legs, along with the chances of over-reaching. The good news is, bowed tendons can be treated, and in most cases, a horse with this condition can be returned to almost complete soundness. Always consult your vet if you suspect a bowed tendon.

Shoeing a horse with a bowed tendon, helping him to be as sound as possible, requires raising the heel. Remember to shoe both front feet the same, regardless of whether both tendons are bowed. Typically, I will use a wedge pad to raise the heels, or I will at least swell the heel of the shoes some to help give the horse more lift in the heel area. It also helps to put a rolled toe on these front shoes, so there is a rounded break-over, rather than an abrupt break-over.

Buck-Kneed

The buck-kneed horse is over in his knees—his legs bow to the front. And generally this horse will be too straight up and down in his feet, because those feet bear more weight over the front. These feet need to be lowered in the heels. This condition is more common in very young horses, and such horses are

very prone to permanent injury if they are used hard before their knee joints have closed up. If a horse still has a tendency toward buck knees by the time he is 3 to 5 years old, he can probably be used without popping a knee.

Calf-Kneed

The calf-kneed horse is behind in his knees. The feet extend too far to the front. Such a horse is prone to becoming run down in his legs. With this condition, the toes need to be kept short, and the heels up, and this will encourage the horse to extend his knees to the front. Extending the heels of the shoes will also give some "lift" to the knees. Generally, calf-kneed horses also have a tendency to splay out pretty badly in their feet, which is a real weakness, so cultivating good feet on these horses is definitely important.

Camped Out and Post-Legged

Camped out and post-legged are similar conditions. Both involve hocks, ankles, and feet that are out of position—set too far behind (camped out), or set too straight (post-legged). Either way , in extreme cases, a horse might not even be able to stand too well. To help such a horse, it is best to lower the heel and maybe extend the toe on the shoe, and cultivate a longer foot. This will help to get the horse more "set under himself," to where he can be used.

Don's Dozen

Here are 12 of my favorite corrective shoes—all of which have stood the test of time. I have used these shoes to cope with a variety of leg and foot problems. Each of these shoes can be made from conventional horseshoes. They should be used in pairs—i.e. a pair on the front feet, or a pair on the back feet, whatever is called for—in order to keep the horse balanced.

Shoe #1
Concave Roller-Motion.
This is effective on founder, navicular, ring-bone, sidebones, and stiff or bad-moving horses. This shoe should be used with side-clips.

Concave

Shoe #2
Clubfooted Shoe.
For horses who grow excessively high heels. This shoe should be applied hot, and burned excessively on the heel. This changes circulation and causes more growth of the toe.

Shoe #3
Calked Ankle.
This shoe can be used with the calk to the outside to help the bow-legged horse. The toe of the shoe should be squared.

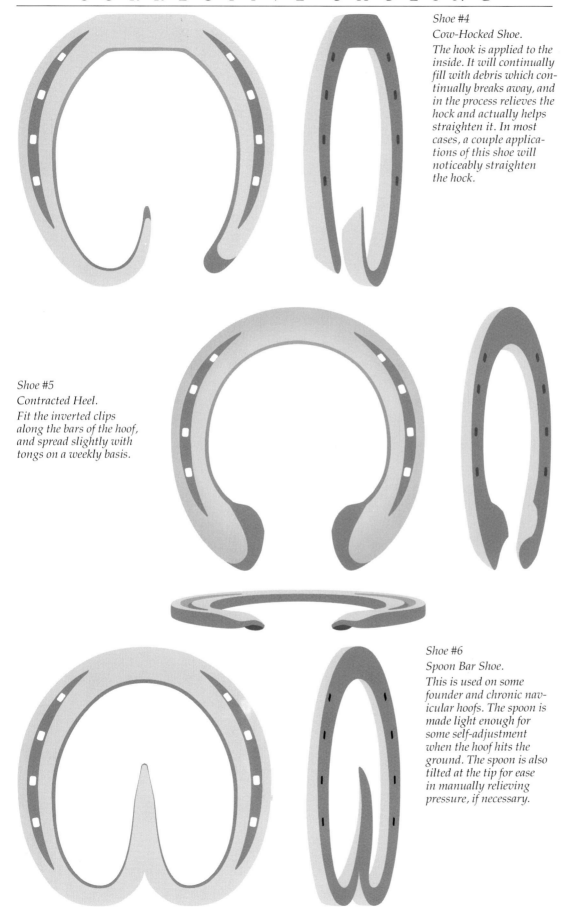

Shoe #4
Cow-Hocked Shoe.
The hook is applied to the inside. It will continually fill with debris which continually breaks away, and in the process relieves the hock and actually helps straighten it. In most cases, a couple applications of this shoe will noticeably straighten the hock.

Shoe #5
Contracted Heel.
Fit the inverted clips along the bars of the hoof, and spread slightly with tongs on a weekly basis.

Shoe #6
Spoon Bar Shoe.
This is used on some founder and chronic navicular hoofs. The spoon is made light enough for some self-adjustment when the hoof hits the ground. The spoon is also tilted at the tip for ease in manually relieving pressure, if necessary.

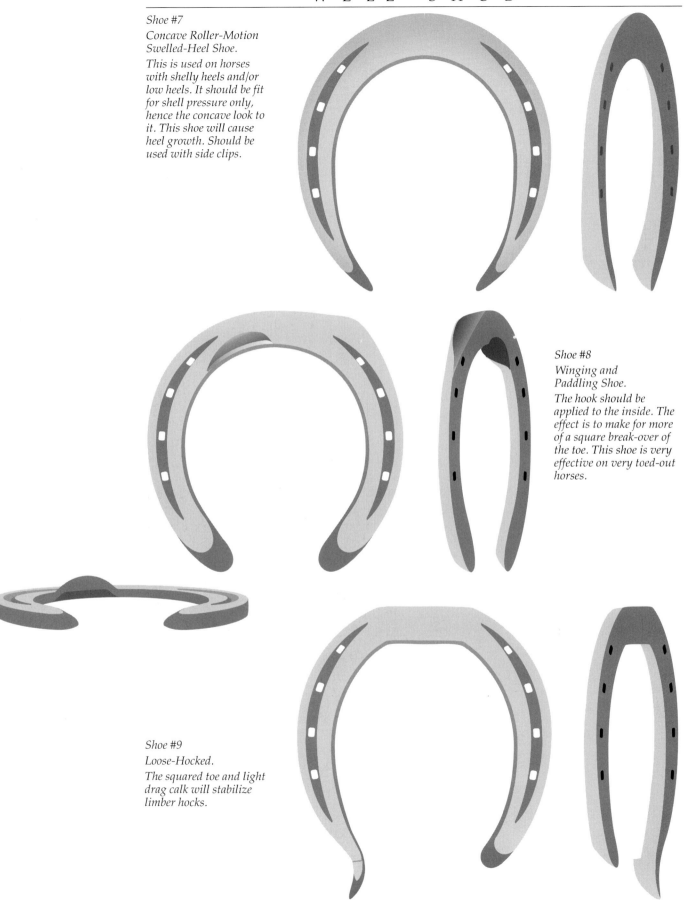

Shoe #7

Concave Roller-Motion Swelled-Heel Shoe.

This is used on horses with shelly heels and/or low heels. It should be fit for shell pressure only, hence the concave look to it. This shoe will cause heel growth. Should be used with side clips.

Shoe #8

Winging and Paddling Shoe.

The hook should be applied to the inside. The effect is to make for more of a square break-over of the toe. This shoe is very effective on very toed-out horses.

Shoe #9

Loose-Hocked.

The squared toe and light drag calk will stabilize limber hocks.

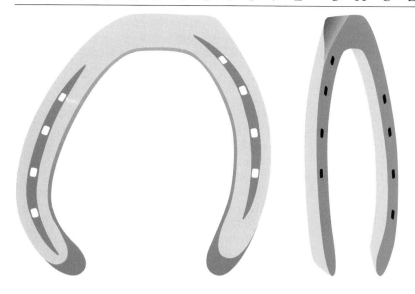

Shoe #10
Bog Spavin.
This should be applied with the straight branch to the inside. The outside should be nailed with two heel nails, and the foot should protrude over the entire shoe. Break in the outside branch from the center of the toe.

Shoe #11
Pigeon-Toed Shoe.
For extremely pigeon-toed horses. The swelled heel goes to the outside of the hoof, the feathered heel to the inside, and the toe should be rolled. The foot should be trimmed low on the inside.

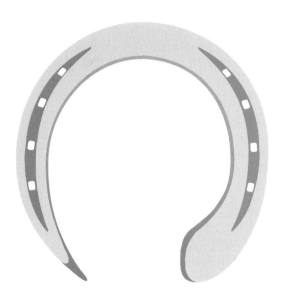

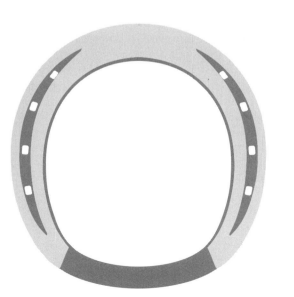

Shoe #12
Egg-Shaped Bar Shoe.
If nothing else works, use this shoe. I use it for bruised bulbs on the heel, broken bars, weak heels, and underslung heels. This shoe is also good for lateral support.

Camped Under

This is the opposite of being camped out. A lot of horses are camped under behind, meaning their feet and hocks are set too far under their hindquarters. The best way to help these horses is to trim off the toes on those hind feet, and grow as much heel as possible. The best shoe to use is the squared-toe with either heel calks, or swelled heels, or extended heels on the shoe to give some lateral support behind.

Corns

Corns are caused by bruises on the sole of the foot, often from ill-fitting shoes, or shoes that were left on too long between shoeings. Typically, they will be around the bars or the wedge of the heel. The best thing to do for a corn is to use the knife to pare it out, and concave the shoe, if necessary, to where there is no sole pressure where the corn was located.

After paring a corn out, I like to heat up an old rasp and burn this area, especially if the corn was fairly large. This will help sear away the remaining area of the corn, and draw the hoof's oil to that area of the foot to aid in healing.

Cow-Hocked

This is the opposite of bow-legged. The hocks are too close to one another, and the feet turn out excessively. In extreme cases, the hocks will even rub against each other while in motion. What I do mainly to fix this condition is to elevate the inside of the foot and trim the outside as low as possible, just the opposite of what I do with a bow-legged horse. Sometimes I will build a long calk on the inside of the foot and run it up along the inside of the bar of the shoe, which provides more elevation to the inside. This helps the hock roll to the outside. And always square the toe on the hind shoes on any of the horses who are really cow-hocked. This gives them more of a square break-over.

On most of the young horses—colts and fillies—cow hocks can be straightened out early simply by trimming. But on the older horses, the farrier finds it necessary to use the lift on the inside and to lower the outside and use a squared-toe shoe. Note the cow-hocked shoe (#4).

Cracks

Quarter cracks are some of the worst cracks. They break downward from the hairline, the coronet band, and it is important to learn how to patch them. Most of the time, I pin quarter cracks, using a couple of number 3 or 3½ racing plate nails to drive across the crack horizontally, one nail in each direction.

I like to heat the nails red hot, so they burn as they go through the shell across the seam or break. By the time I am ready to clinch both nails and finish them off, the burning has drawn a natural oil to the area and makes the foot more flexible, to where it will more readily accept the pulling together of the crack. This burning also serves to help sterilize the nails, and thus prevent the start of a low-grade infection. A tetanus shot and antibiotics might also be called for in treating this kind of condition. A veterinarian can advise. I start the nails about ½ inch on each side of the crack, at a bevel, because the nails are going in horizontally to the rounded hoof.

Most of the time, a horse with a severe quarter crack that has not been attended to will bleed from the crack if he is used. Sometimes such a crack will require the application of a couple of stainless-steel screws. The shell may be too thin to nail. In that case, I will drill a hole on either side of the crack—about ¼-inch deep, then start a screw in each hole. As soon as each hole is threaded, I will back the screws out and cut them off from the bottom, so they are the proper length to go in the holes. Leave enough of the screw head on each to anchor a piece of wire, which will stretch across the crack to hold it together, and prevent it from widening. Then tighten the screws down until snug.

Next step: The area should be covered with fiberglass or one of the special hoof sealants that are on the market for purposes such as this.

I have also used a copper plate and stainless-steel screws with about eight or ten holes in the plate drilled and countersunk for the screws.

Sometimes, a horse will get a long foot, step on a rock wrong, and break off a heel. This makes for a very bad quarter crack.

Quarter cracks are some of the worst cracks, and it is important to learn how to patch them.

114

Various Cracks, Cuts, and Patches

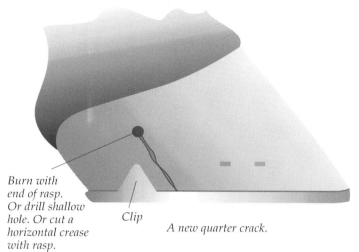

Burn with
end of rasp.
Or drill shallow
hole. Or cut a
horizontal crease
with rasp.

Clip

A new quarter crack.

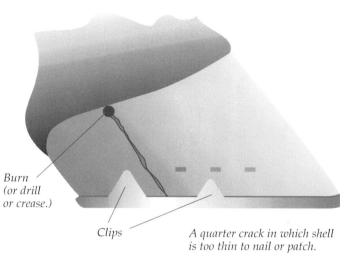

Burn
(or drill
or crease.)

Clips

A quarter crack in which shell
is too thin to nail or patch.

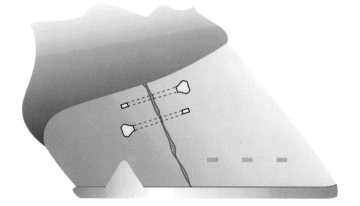

Nailing a quarter crack.

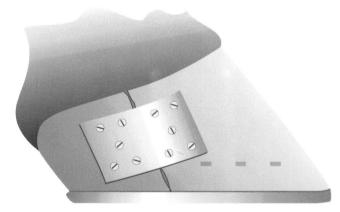

Copper patch with stainless steel screws—
used on a quarter crack.

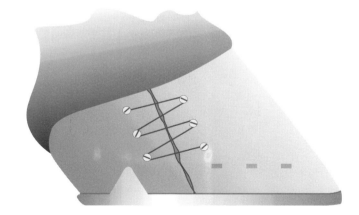

Fixing a quarter crack with piano wire and screws.
A Fiberglas patch should then cover the area.

⅜"   ¼"

Thread the hole with the ⅜-inch
screw, but do not put screw all
the way in. Back it out, cut off
the point, and use the screw as
a ¼-inch screw.

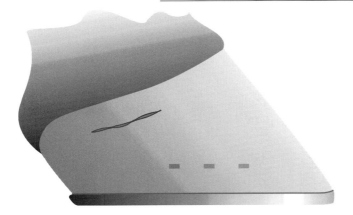

Parallel crack. Keep an eye on it. No special treatment called for at this time. Crack will gradually grow out and disappear.

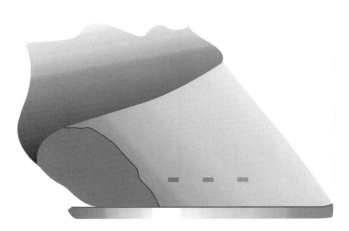

Heel torn away. Hoof can be shod after wound has dried. Heel will grow back in about 6 months.

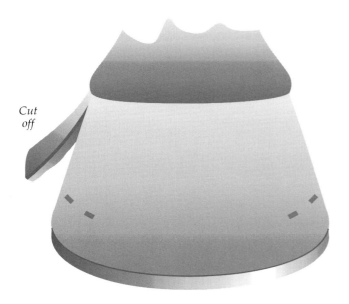

Cut off

Broken heel. Cut off with nippers, dress with rasp, burn area, apply bar shoe.

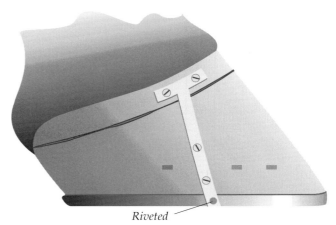

Riveted

Extensive injury at coronet band, now working its way down the hoof. This type of support can be helpful.

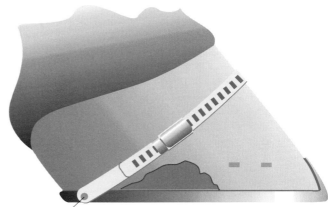

Riveted (drill hole through side of shoe, and use 8-penny nail for rivet).

Hoof torn away

Hose band—used in place of nail.

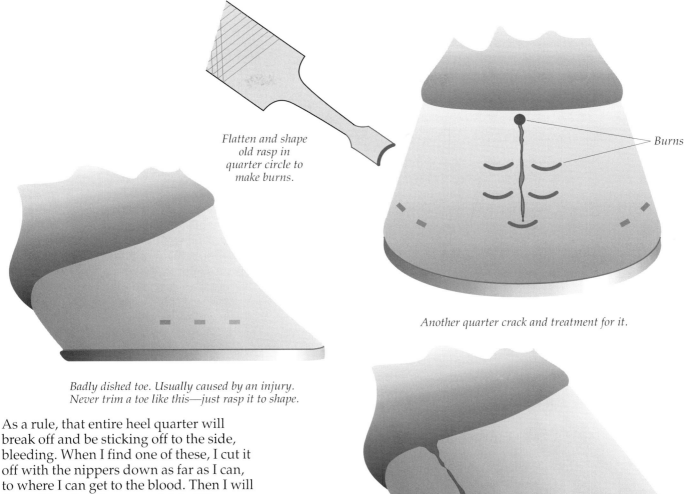

Flatten and shape old rasp in quarter circle to make burns.

Burns

Another quarter crack and treatment for it.

Badly dished toe. Usually caused by an injury. Never trim a toe like this—just rasp it to shape.

Wire cut or cut in coronet band. Scar never goes away, but foot remains strong.

As a rule, that entire heel quarter will break off and be sticking off to the side, bleeding. When I find one of these, I cut it off with the nippers down as far as I can, to where I can get to the blood. Then I will dress this off with a rasp. A lot of times, this will be maybe an inch higher than the rest of the foot.

These bad heel breaks are hard to grow back, and as a rule we have to go with a bar shoe on the horse to hold the foot together so it can grow out.

If a horse breaks a heel, and the whole heel section turns out, and is bleeding, and the inside of the foot is visible, I will take a hot rasp and burn the area. In a few days, this will harden up and the horse will be sound enough with a bar shoe to where he will be useable. Sometimes, too, a regular shoe can be used and turned up to give the horse some lateral support where the quarter is broken out of his foot.

Most real bad breaks like this occur in Thoroughbreds or Thoroughbred-crosses. The shells of their feet are a little thinner than in other breeds. Most Quarter Horses and Arabians have a heavier shell, and there is little of this problem associated with them.

More cracks: A lot of horses will get a little parallel crack in the foot, and this generally comes from the top of the hair-line down. What causes this is a small piece of gravel that has worked its way up the foot and come out at the coronet band. At that point, there is a slight infection that develops, and the horse is generally sore from it for 2 or 3 days, until the gravel has worked out. And then the coronet band and hoof grow down, and that is where the little parallel crack comes from. There will be evidence of this crack on the bottom of the hoof too.

Other cracks, parallel or vertical (quarter cracks), can form at the base of the hoof and begin to work their way upward. Hoofs that are very dry are especially prone to cracks like this, as are feet that have been neglected —hoofs that have not been trimmed when they needed trimming, or shoes left on longer than they should have been. For dry hoofs, a hoof dressing will help.

A farrier can help keep any of these cracks from spreading, from moving all the way up or down a hoof, by scoring above and/or below the crack, whether the crack is horizontal or vertical. Scoring means taking the rasp and cutting a thin little groove into the hoof. If a crack is working its way down from the top, score above the crack, or at least as near to the top of the crack as possible, without getting into the hairline. And then score immediately below the crack, to interrupt its downward progression. If the crack is coming from the bottom of the hoof, score immediately above the crack. Heating the tang of a rasp and burning the score above and/or below a crack, whatever is called for, is yet another effective method for preventing the crack's progression. The burn, of course, draws the natural oil of the foot to the surface and aids in healing.

Most of these surface cracks will not show in the bottom of the foot through the shell when we are paring the foot down. They will be only in the surface of the shell. And so there is little in the way of a big problem that can result from these types of cracks.

Founder

A horse who has foundered is better off going barefooted, if possible. A year without shoes, but with regular trimming, will allow the horse to wear off his feet more naturally and drive the quick back inside his foot. Whenever the foundered horse is shod, there is a tendency for him to pull away from his toe, and to bear more weight on the heel. The tendency is to grow excessive heel and to get a dish in the toe. It is therefore important to keep the toe rasped down and rolled severely, and at the same time work on keeping the heel from growing excessively.

However, severely foundered horses who are trying to recover are often so sore on their front feet that shoeing will help relieve some of the pain. There are a couple of shoes that work well on the foundered horse, and they are the con-

cave roller-motion shoe with side clips (#1), and the spoon-bar shoe (#6). This latter is a variation of the heart-bar shoe, but the difference is that one can vary the pressure, somewhat, that the spoon is applying to the sole, pushing against the coffin bone, encouraging it to rotate back into a normal position. The pain comes from the coffin bone trying to push down through the sole.

However, another procedure that I have been using recently on foundered horses, and find to be very effective, is to use a common cedar-wood roof shingle, the kind that is tapered in the shape of a wedge, and use that in conjunction with a neoprene or leather pad on a shoe. The shingle is cut to the width of the interior of the foot, and driven between the pad and the sole.

The cedar shingle will do nothing to harm the foot, and can be adjusted—either pulling it back out a ways, or driving it farther in for increased pressure—according to how much pressure is needed against the sole. The right amount of pressure is what gives the horse some pain relief, and helps push the coffin bone back into place.

A horse can founder from a variety of things—drinking too much water when he is very hot, reactions to medication, eating too much green grass or grain, and he can road-founder too. The latter may come from being overworked on pavement or hard ground, with the resulting concussion causing founder. A horse is also susceptible to road founder if he is freshly shod, and then taken on a long, cross-country trailer trip. Sometimes people do not know their horse has foundered; they just know he is suddenly very sore in his feet.

At any rate, this procedure using the cedar shingle and the pad has helped a lot of horses through founder from all of the above causes. A horse who has survived the initial founder, and has stabilized, might also do well with a bowed rocker shoe. This is a regular shoe with rolled toe and heel.

Bowed rocker shoe.

Sometimes we find a horse (or pony, mule, or donkey) who has been foundered on all four feet and has excessive hoof growth. These animals will need to be pared down about three to four times a year. These feet grow uncontrollably, and without trimming can quickly get a four- to six-inch "horn" on the front of each foot. The heels will be pulled clear underneath, and the horse will be walking with these deformed feet rolled up in the front.

To trim a foot like this, start at the point of the heel, which is out there in front, and start cutting back and beveling through the extra growth behind the heel. You will reach a point where the heel will be back in touch with the ground. At that point, take a hacksaw and saw off the excess toe. It could be several inches or more of excessive growth around the toe.

After this has been done, the nippers and hoof knife can be used to pare the sole and frog out, and then the toe should be rolled. Then animal has a foot that is somewhat normal, at least for a while. This excessive growth from this type of foundered condition never ceases. I have had animals I have taken care of with this for 20 years, and they still grow it. Naturally, the animals are not really useful, but they are pets to their owners, who want to continue to care for them and have their feet pared down, rather than put them down.

If these feet are cut down regularly, such animals do not show signs of stress or pain. They will grow the most foot when it is wet, or if they are on green grass. Wheat pasture is extremely bad for an animal in this condition. Ideally, such a foundered animal should be kept in a dry lot, or allowed only in a pasture with dry, cured grass. Such an animal should never be shod.

Fractured Sole

When this occurs, it is usually to a young horse—a colt, yearling, or 2-year-old—and the horse is usually in a dry, rocky country. The sole sheds out, as nature intended, and the new growth underneath can be soft and somewhat vulnerable to sharp rocks for a while—this is one cause. Sometimes, I think the foot spreads out and the sole does not have enough elasticity in it to accommodate the spread, and so it breaks.

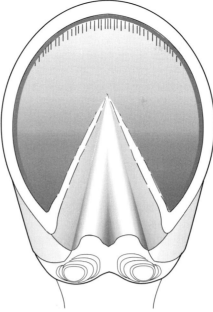

Very contracted heels.

Evidence of a light founder will reveal a little seedy toe. Perhaps there was no rotation of the coffin bone. However, most founders will also show contracted heels. Even though a heel is contracted, it may still grow excessively, and need to be trimmed off regularly. Sometimes a foundered horse will show excessive heel growth and little toe growth.

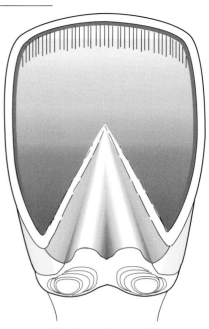

Club foot or box-toed foot.

This illustration shows a boxed toe (or club foot) with seedy toe present. A club foot is invariably the result of injury, and is predisposed to founder, just as navicular predisposes a foot to founder. Seedy toe goes along with founder. It is tough material and does not wear off, but continues to grow to the front and pulls the frog forward in the process. The seedy toe causes the outside shell of the foot to thicken, and this is what causes the toe to dish.

Shingle or wood wedge

Shingle under wedge pad.

A fractured sole occurs invariably in a front foot, rarely in a back foot, and it usually breaks in three sections. Sometimes the break is bad enough to bleed and cause an abscess. While most broken soles will heal on their own in about 5 to 8 weeks, especially if the horse is rested and moved to softer ground (perhaps a meadow instead of a rocky pasture), the horse will still be extremely sore during this time. The best thing to do for the horse, to help the sole heal, is to put shoes and pads on both front feet, even if only one foot has the fractured sole. The good foot will need protection, too, because the horse is apt to use it more to compensate for the sore foot, and may wind up with two fractured soles, otherwise.

For extreme cases, it is beneficial to pack the foot with Reducine before applying the pad and shoe. The Reducine will help the sole to grow back more quickly and more thickly, it seals the sole, to keep air out of the area, and there is a good chance that the horse will walk away sound after this treatment. Another trick to use on this type of injury is to clip the coronary band and apply iodine to that area. This causes more circulation in the foot, which stimulates growth and helps bring the horse back to soundness more quickly.

Last but not least, the veterinarian should be consulted for antibiotic treatment to help guard against infection.

Frog and Sole Bound

This is a condition in which the frog and sole grow together. It is bad for the horse because it renders the hoof relatively inflexible, inhibiting the flow of blood out of the foot and causing soreness.

To correct the situation, I get an old rasp, heat the end of it so I can sharpen it on the anvil, then heat it some more and use that hot, sharpened end to cut free the sides of the frog from the sole. This immediately puts some flexibility back into the foot, and it will open up from $1/2$ to $3/4$ of an inch.

For horses who are contracted in the heels, and the heel is pulled under the hoof, it is real good to use this same hot rasp to cut the frog loose from the bars and the heel of the foot. The foot should be flexible enough so you can take the palms of your hands and squeeze against the sides of the foot and see the frog open and close slightly with the give and take of pressure.

Sometimes we find that the bars have grown curled around into the frog. Again, this inhibits healthy foot growth and creates soreness. Rasping a wedge out of that bar, where it is curled around into the frog, will give a horse relief and cause the foot to function more properly and to grow normally. More information: page 131.

Hip Capped

This refers to a horse who has had his hip cap knocked down from some type of injury. The injured leg will generally wither somewhat, and get a little shorter than the other leg. To help a horse with this condition, I leave more foot and heel on the *good* foot, maybe $3/8$ths to $1/2$-inch longer than the other, and I shoe both hind feet with squared-toe shoes. The reason for the difference in the amount of foot left on the two hind feet is to relieve stress, somewhat, on the injured leg. Trying to "build up" the injured leg by shoeing it equally with the other will put more stress in that hip and cause the horse to be lame. Shoeing the two differently in this manner will generally enable the horse to stay sound and functional. Looking at such a horse from behind, one can see the injured hip is permanently lowered 1 to 2 inches compared to the good hip.

Locoweed

Sometimes, a horseshoer will encounter a "weedy" horse, one who has been eating locoweed to the point where it has permanently damaged his brain. The problem, quite often, is most severe in the spring—locoweed is usually the first plant to green-up in a pasture after winter. Once horses develop a taste for locoweed, they will search it out, and that is when the damage occurs.

Unfortunately for the unsuspecting rider or farrier, such a horse may not show outward signs of being locoed. The horseshoer may get three feet shod, and suddenly the horse will blow up for no reason, and just appear to have lost his mind. If you go ahead and get such a horse shod, but suspect by then that he is weedy or locoed, by all means tell the owner, who may not realize what is going on with the horse. If you know a horse is weedy beforehand, do not attempt to shoe him at all.

Some people believe such a horse can be "fed out of it (the condition)", by keeping the horse in a pen and feeding him hay. Yes, the horse will get a little better, but when he gets hot through work or any other stress, that is when the condition will manifest itself again. Such a locoed horse becomes dangerous and unpredictable to be around or to ride—spooking, running off, becoming suddenly rank.

There are a few tell-tale signs to be aware of with this condition. One is if a horse walks up to a water tank and sticks his head clear down in the water, maybe up to his eyes, and just stands there. The horse might even drown. If you go to a place and see a horse in a pen with a watertank that has a float-valve set to allow only 4 inches of water in the tank, there is a good chance the owner has a locoed horse he is trying to deal with. Other possible signs—the horse might be a little too "silly" about his feet and his head, refuse to walk through a barn door, or to go under a low shed.

Again, there is no point in even attempting to shoe such a horse.

Low Heels

A horse with low heels, in which the heels do not seem to grow down, but rather grow forward, under the feet, needs some help in the form of a swelled heel shoe. To make this I put the shoe in the fire and then thicken, or elevate, the heel of the shoe. This redistributes the weight and promotes healthy growth of the entire foot.

Another shoe that works good on low heels is the lateral support shoe, a shoe that is a couple sizes too big for the horse, affording room to turn the shoe heels upward, to support the heel of the foot.

Conversely, if a horse tends to grow too much heel, I will flatten out the heel of the shoe and cover the back of the foot over the bar, and that will keep the foot from growing excessively. Sometimes I will even burn the heel with the hot shoe, driving the blood back up into the foot, then rasp off more heel before applying the flat

shoe. But, any way you look at it, it is a lot harder to promote more heel growth than it is to deal with too much heel growth.

Something else that promotes heel growth is to shear the coronet band with clippers, then use 7 percent iodine to put a blister on the coronet band. This stimulates circulation in the hoof, and will make it grow. You can promote growth of the entire foot by blistering the entire coronet band, not just the areas back around the heels. The iodine could go on once a day for 3 days, then off for 3 days, and then on once a day for 3 more days, and that should do it. If you can make the foot grow, then you can help shape the foot to where the horse has more of a balanced foundation under him.

And speaking of general hoof growth, water is a pretty good aid in this process. In a dry country, something as simple as maintaining a little mud around a water tank can really help with moisture in a horse's feet, and that in turn promotes good circulation in the feet and good growth.

Navicular Disease

This disease, unfortunately, is far too common, and is progressive and incurable. It is caused by strain around the navicular bone inside the hoof, and starts out as a bursitis that, over a period of months and years, becomes degenerative and causes the horse to go lamer and lamer. Navicular is usually in both front feet, but one foot may be affected more than the other. Early symptoms include lameness that a horse seems to "warm out of" as he is exercised. The gait will be short and choppy, and the horse may "point" one or

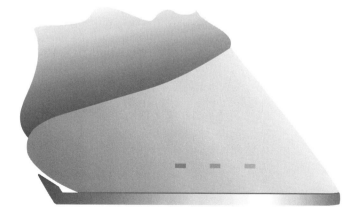

Dropped heel with lateral support shoe.

A variety of conditions are caused by bone or joint inflammation.

both feet to the side, while standing, as he tries to relieve the pain. The navicular foot will tend to shrink in size and become brittle, as time goes on, and the heel will become contracted. The sole and frog will shrink, as well.

Veterinary diagnosis and treatment, in conjunction with corrective shoeing, will help prolong the useful life of a navicular horse. The concave roller-motion shoe (#1) and the spoon bar shoe (#6) are both effective on chronic navicular hoofs. First choice is the concave roller-motion shoe with a sideclip on each side, to firm up that foot. This shoe will usually help most navicular horses. I have found, by looking at veterinary X-rays of these feet before shoeing and then 6 months after being shod regularly with this type of shoe, that the concave roller-motion shoe even seems to slow down or somewhat reverse (temporarily, at least) the degeneration that causes the lameness. This shoe with the rolled toe makes it easier—less stressful and therefore less painful—for the horse to break over with every step he takes. Sometimes, it also helps such a horse to use a 2-degree wedge pad in conjunction with this shoe.

Occasionally, horses with navicular or other chronic foot problems (a broken coffin bone, perhaps) that cause lameness, are *nerved*. A veterinarian operates above the area, around the pastern, to clip nerves to the diseased portion of the foot. For horses who have been nerved, I definitely like to roll their toes slightly and put them in a 2-degree wedge pad for the first couple shoeings after surgery. Again, the rolled toe helps with the breakover, and the wedge pad helps lift the heel, which has a tendency to break down, or atrophy somewhat following surgery. The horse can be shod normally with an open shoe by about the third shoeing following nerving.

For these horses, it is best to not restrict their feet with the wrong kind of shoes. Putting them in a bar shoe or eggbar shoe would be unwise. Because nerving has a tendency to make the foot less flexible than it was before, it is important to encourage the foot to have as much contact with the ground as possible, so it can maintain circulation and have more live feel to it.

Periostitis and Osteoarthritis

These are the medical terms that define a variety of conditions described below. Periostitis is inflammation of the membrane covering the bone, eventually resulting in the outgrowth of new bone, and osteoarthritis refers to inflammation of a joint, with eventual outgrowth of new bone. One or the other of these conditions, or a combination of both conditions, brought about by injury, are what cause things like curb bone, osselets, popped knee, ringbone, shinbucks, sidebone, and splints. These conditions can often be avoided with prompt treatment following injury, and such treatment often involves icing down the area initially, combined with rest, and veterinary treatment (especially in cases that are not attended to promptly).

Curb Bone

The curb bones are on the hind legs, and are roughly the counterparts to splints on the front legs, except that they are a single bone, one on the outside of each leg, extending below the hock. The curb bones become bruised and enlarged generally from the stress of stopping and backing up too much. Soreness from curb bones can be alleviated by elevating the heels and letting the toes down on the hind feet. This will relieve some of the stress to those areas.

Osselets

This is a condition common in race horses, brought on by excessive stress, in this case to the ankle area (specifically, the front of the pastern region). This condition is most easily noticed when one picks up the foot and notices a creaky sensation when the ankle area is moved. Generally, there will be swelling, especially in the back of the joint. Sometimes this is caused by a hard bump—maybe the horse bumped his ankles together, bruised the osselet area, and this is what created the fluid buildup. Time off and rest seem to be essential for any healing to take place. Persistent cases result in stiffness and chronic pain.

Popped Knee

This is the condition in which a horse is injured in the knee joint and develops fluid in the area which, if left untreated, can leave the horse unsound. A large calcium deposit will form in the shape of a knot on the knee, generally on the outside of the joint. As a rule, such a horse will stand somewhat toed out with that leg. Permanent damage to the knee or other joints that are injured can often be avoided with prompt icing on and off for a day, immediately following the injury. Consult a veterinarian for best results.

Ringbone

Faulty conformation (toeing in, toeing out, pasterns that are too short and straight) can predispose a horse to ringbone, but the ringbone itself is brought about by excessive stress or some other external injury to the ankle area. High ringbone is a calcium growth in the pastern area, and this may or may not cause a lameness problem. Low ringbone is within the hoof, and will invariably need an X-ray to determine exactly what is causing lameness in the early stages. With low ringbone, the coronet starts to bulge as the condition worsens. If ringbone is diagnosed soon enough, it can often be cured with rest, sometimes in the form of a cast, and anti-inflammatory drugs.

The concave roller-motion shoe (#1) is most effective for a horse with a history of ringbone.

Shinbucks

Shinbucked horses are found generally at the racetrack. The condition results in a soreness and slight swelling along the cannon bone between the knee and ankle, typically on young horses. Most of these horses were worked too hard on legs that are too immature. In addition to the hard work on the track, these horses are often improperly shod with a shoe that is too long on a hoof that was left too long and with a heel that is too low. Correcting the shoeing, coupled with rest, will cure bucked shins.

Sidebone

Sidebones may or may not cause lameness. They typically are located on the sides of the front feet, back toward the heels and above the coronets. Normally,

these are cartilages. If injured, they can calcify, and then they are called sidebones. Sometimes a sidebone will connect with a ringbone, and cause serious lameness. As with ringbone, the most relief one can give a horse with this type of problem is to use the concave roller-motion shoe (#1).

The shoe provides the horse with a smooth breakover, where he does not have the stress through his coronary band that he would with a shoe that was flat on the end of his toe, causing a sharp breakover.

Splints

These are bony enlargements of the splint bones on the sides of the front legs, between ankles and knees. The enlargements come from injury, typically by striking the area with another foot. Splints are fairly common on young horses, and some "go away" on their own. Others need time off from riding or training to heal.

Splints generally occur on the inside, below the knee. Seldom will one appear on the outside of the leg, but it can happen there, too. If a splint is at least ½ inch below the knee, I have found there is generally little to be concerned about. If the enlargement extends into the knee, it is probably best to consult a veterinarian. At the very least, the horse will need to be laid up and not used. If the splint bone is fractured, it may need to be removed surgically.

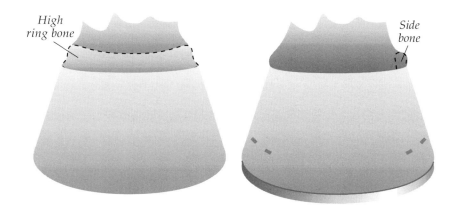

High ring bone

Side bone

Puncture Wounds

Perhaps the most common cause of lameness in horses is a nail in the foot. The galvanized roofing nails or sheet metal screws are the worst. If a horse comes up lame, this is the first thing to check for. Whenever I see a horse with a raw, bloody break at the back of the heel, I will clean out his foot, and as a rule, laying along the frog or in some section of the foot will be a nail puncture, or the nail itself. A tetanus shot and antibiotics are the usual treatment for a wound like this; and perhaps also soaking the foot in epsom salts and warm water several times a day for a week. A veterinarian should be consulted.

Rope Walking

The term rope walking means a horse is traveling real close in front, and/or behind, putting one foot in the same line of travel as the other, as though he was walking a rope with his feet. With a horse like this, the farrier needs to lower the feet on the inside. As a rule, that will spread the hocks and knees so one leg doesn't bump against the other.

A squared-toe shoe applied on front and back feet generally helps give the horse a square break-over instead of breaking over the inside (or outside). On the front shoes, I do not square them real abruptly, but fit them wider and maybe take the point of each shoe to the outside slightly, to give them a little more breakover, and to keep those feet from rolling over the inside and getting too close to one another.

I may also use what I call a drag calk on these horses who want to rope walk. It will elevate the outside heel where it has a tendency to make that horse stand in a wider pattern behind. To make this drag calk, use a shoe with longer branches than

you need. Make the calk on the outside of the shoe, turning the outside branch under itself and blocking it so it winds up being a calk about an inch long and about $3/8$ths of an inch thick. Cut off the inside branch to a normal length, so the shoe is an even length on both sides, only slightly longer, with the calk under the outside branch. This shoe should be used on both hind feet.

Run Down

When one hears of a horse being run down, it is usually a horse at the racetrack. This can happen in both front and hind feet, but it is usually worse in the hind. This is a suspensory problem—the horse is weak in his pasterns, and his suspensories stretch enough from the stress of hard running to where his ankles will be nearly on the ground. The condition is further brought about by low heels and long toes, and the addition of calks on the shoes.

For horses like this who are still at the track, it is best to make them egg-bar shoes—and probably put the shoes on backwards to give the horses enough support to keep from burning their ankles on the racetrack turf.

For horses with this condition who are off the track and doing something else, like barrel racing, reining, or roping, it is best to work on elevating those feet with shoes and pads. As a rule, most run-down horses are worse in the back feet. It is easy to put a good block heel on the hind shoes, so try that. If more elevation is needed in the heels, a wedge pad can be used with both hind shoes. The use of skid boots also lessens the chance of burning the pasterns on those hind feet during a hard run and/or stop. I have seen some horses who were also bandaged up in the ankle areas prior to use, just to give those areas extra support.

I have had success on some run-down horses by using a wide sliding plate with a long trailer. This puts extra weight and extra length on their feet with this type of shoe, and the idea is this extra weight and length strengthens those tendons and helps the horse to get more upright in his ankles.

Scalping

Scalping (also called speed cutting) refers to the condition in which a horse reaches forward and across with a hind foot, and hits the opposite front ankle, cutting it. Scalping can occur when a horse is running, and for that reason it is common at the racetrack. A horse is prone to having this happen when he is ridden on the wrong lead in a turn, or is cross-firing, or is running kind of wildly, and not in a collected manner.

The best shoeing for a horse with this type of problem is the same as that used for the rope-walker, described earlier. Use square-toed shoes on the front and back, and have an outside calk on both back shoes. The calk gives the shoe a little more weight to the outside, and when the hind foot comes off the ground, it will tilt the heel down a little with that extra weight of the calk, and therefore let the foot come forward but at a slightly wider path of travel, thus missing the front foot. The squared toes in front also promote a faster breakover in the front feet, allowing them to get out of the ground a bit quicker, and thus out of the way of the back feet.

Scratches

This is a fungus-type problem that results in rough, raw areas that form just above the bulbs of the feet on horses. It can be hard to cure, and in extreme cases make the horse lame. I have found that anything with an iodine base to it seems to help cure this condition, as long as the dressing is not greasy. Something else that seems to work in conjunction with the iodine solution (not straight iodine) is not working the horse and keeping him in a clean pen or pasture until the condition clears up.

Short-Strided

One can do a lot with the different weights of shoes that are available. Most Quarter Horses and Thoroughbreds cannot carry excessive weight on their feet, but can easily carry a shoe that is 6 to 8 ounces. For a horse who seems to be somewhat short-strided, I will fit him with shoes that are a little heavier than what he has been carrying, and will draw the heels (lengthen the heels with forge and anvil) to give him a little more lift in each foot.

Sickle-Hocked

Sickle hocks are another conformation problem the farrier must deal with in horses. The condition is so-named because the hind legs resemble a sickle—the horse is generally camped out behind in his hocks, but the hind feet are set too far under, too close to the front feet. This puts a pretty direct bend in the hock area, and the extra stress in that area often can lead to problems like bog spavin.

The best way to fix these feet is to grow some heel on the horse, use a squared-toe shoe on those hind feet, and extend the shoe out a little behind. This creates some elevation and lateral support in those legs that will make this type of horse stand up better. The sickle-hocked horse is prone to interfere with his front feet, and that is another reason for the squared-toe shoe on the hind feet.

Inadequate nutrition seems to play a part in the formation of sickle hocks in foals. If the farrier can start working on such a foal, and the veterinarian can straighten out his nutrition, this condition can be corrected to a point as the foal matures. On older horses, if the farrier does not have time to cultivate heel growth, he can use a $3/8$th- or $1/2$-inch wedge pad on those hind feet to get some elevation to where the horse can be used.

As I said, there is extra stress on the hind legs in the sickle-hocked horse, but the condition does not seem to cause a lot of discomfort in the horse most of the time. I have known some sickle-hocked horses who performed very well in calf roping—they could certainly stop hard, built that way. But this type of horse does seem to be uncomfortable when asked to pick up a hind foot for trimming and shoeing. There is more stress on the farrier when shoeing this type of horse too.

What I often do with a horse like this, who is reluctant to let me pick up a hind foot, is to maneuver him to a wall, where I can get him to lean against the wall, and then I pull that hind foot forward and try to get the stifle muscle to relax so I can then position that foot to work on it. I may need to pick this foot up three or four times before the horse relaxes enough to let me work on it. These horses are not mean about their feet, but I think it may hurt them to stand on one hind leg like that.

Generally, I can get a hind foot trimmed, let it down, go adjust the shoe, then come back and probably drive two or three nails before I have to let the foot down again. This type of horse is still very serviceable with proper shoeing, and I believe he can go ahead and do his work without pain.

Sore Knees

Horses with front feet that were trimmed improperly, left high on the outside of the hoofs, are prone to developing soreness in their knees. They will also not travel as fluidly as they should. The answer is to lower the outside of the hoofs and leave a little more inside toe.

Spavin

There are several types of spavins that a farrier will run across in his shoeing rounds, and they are noticed as swelled areas around the hock. They may be caused by strains, improper nutrition, or faulty conformation. A *blood spavin* is simply an enlarged vein that runs across the front of the hock, and while it is a blemish, it does not cause any lameness. A *bog spavin*, on the other hand, is a fairly large swelling in the front of the hock, and it is filled with fluid from the joint. Additional related bulges may be seen on the sides of the hock. Bog spavins can be treated successfully by a veterinarian, especially if treated early on. A period of rest is usually called for.

Bone spavin, however, is a bony, arthritic enlargement on the hock joint, and such spavins are commonly called "jacks." The cause is strain and injury, and horses with faulty conformation in the back legs are predisposed to this. Jacks cause lameness and do not respond to veterinary treatment, but there are some things a farrier can do in the way of corrective shoeing to keep such a horse serviceable. The spavin shoe (#10) is what I use on such a horse. The straight side of the shoe goes to the inside of the foot. The outside should be nailed with two heel nails and the foot should protrude over the entire shoe. The break in the outside branch of the shoe should start from the center of the toe.

Stifle

A horse can get stifled if he slips in the hindquarters and the tendon over the stifle cap gets stretched. This causes the horse pain, and the stifle joint will not stay located in the socket it is meant to be in.

The farrier can help a stifled horse heal by fitting his opposite hind foot—not the one that has the stifle problem—with a stifle shoe. This is a shoe with an arch in it, about $1\frac{1}{2}$ inches high, formed by welding

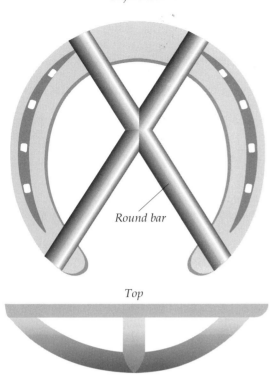

Stifle shoe.

Round bar

Top

a flat cross-bar to the shoe from the point of the heel to the toe. Elevating the opposite foot lessens stress on the stifled leg, reduces discomfort or pain, and encourages the horse to use that stifled leg more as it heals. Using the stifled leg instead of carrying it also promotes healing.

Some horses show a tendency to lock up in both stifles for no apparent reason—in other words, they have not been injured—and this is a genetic problem. Such a horse either cannot back up or has great difficulty backing. A veterinarian should be consulted, because the condition can be remedied or at least greatly relieved through medical treatment that may involve a series of injections in the stifles, or perhaps clipping the tendon involved with that joint. Working with the farrier, the vet will probably also recommend elevating the heels on the hind feet, and squaring the toes.

String-Halt

This condition is characterized by the horse abruptly and abnormally jerking a hind leg up to his belly as he walks. It is caused by an injury to a tendon in the leg, perhaps a nick on the tendon in front of the hock. This used to be somewhat common on horses who had to pull heavy loads, and were more at risk of injuring themselves in this way while working. Today, there are relatively few string-halted horses around that anyone is trying to use.

To help a horse with this condition, put him in roller-motion shoes, keep some extra heel on his feet, and roll the toes, so he does not have an abrupt breakover. This seems to keep some tension off that damaged tendon, and makes it so he does not jerk his leg up so abruptly. Shod this way, a string-halted horse may be feasible to use. One thing to be careful of: When picking up the affected foot for trimming and shoeing, the foot may jump into your hand, perhaps driving your thumb out of joint. Use caution when picking up a foot like this.

Swelling in Hocks

For most horses with swelling in their hocks, the cause is generally improper trimming. Invariably, their hind feet have been left too high on the outsides. The answer, as it was in sore knees, is to let the outside down and leave a little more inside toe, and generally the swelling in the hock will go down within 3 or 4 days.

Tail Wringing

A horse who constantly wrings or flicks his tail is showing signs of being bothered by something physically—he is in some

127

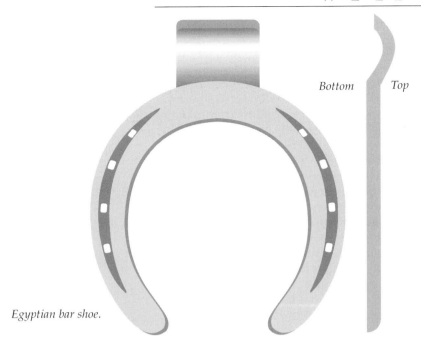

Bottom   *Top*

Egyptian bar shoe.

degree of pain or frustration caused by his rider. Pain can be caused by the bit, faulty equipment (like an ill-fitting saddle or a saddle with a broken tree), or the way he is shod, or the way he is built, or some combination of the above, or by spurring.

Bow-legged and cow-hocked horses are especially prone to this problem while being worked. As a rule, getting those hocks stabilized and getting the horse comfortable behind will make the tail wringing stop. We can watch a horse's ears and watch his tail, and be able to tell if we have him shod properly.

If the horse continues to be bad about wringing his tail, and we believe he is shod properly, then the search for the cause must continue. I have been to places where the owner says his horse is sound, other than when he is ridden. Many times

in situations like that, a close look at the saddle will reveal a broken tree the owner was not aware of. The weight of a rider will make that tree pinch the horse somewhere on his back or around his withers, and may cause him to not only swish his tail, but to travel lame. Dirty cinches and saddle pads can also make for a sore-backed horse.

Tendon Severed

Occasionally, we are asked to help a horse who has severed a suspensory tendon in a leg. This type of injury does not lend itself to being sewed together again by a veterinarian, but a vet should still be consulted. Invariably, the "prescription" will call for something to prevent the foot from flexing too much, and thus interfering with healing. The idea is for the tendon, though it is cut, to heal to the point where it calcifies and thickens so it will still provide some support to the foot.

I like to use an Egyptian bar shoe on a horse with this injury. This shoe is made with a spoon on the front of it, rolled up. I generally take an old rasp and weld about 2 or 2½ inches of it on the end of the shoe, and roll it up so this horse can carry it and not be able to roll his foot over.

Reminder: Special shoes like this should always be used in pairs, for front feet (if one of the front feet is injured), and for hind feet (if one of the hind feet is injured). A horse will adapt to a strange shoe like this, and recover more quickly from the injury, if both the injured foot and uninjured foot are shod the same.

This shoe was developed by Egyptians for horses who work in sand constantly. It literally helps a horse in those conditions to not wear out his feet. We have found it to be a good therapeutic shoe for this and similar types of injuries. I have also used it on colts who have a boxed toe, or club foot. This shoe makes the colt extend himself and changes the circulation in the foot, to where he will probably grow out of the condition and be useable.

Another shoe I use on a horse with a cut suspensory is a counter-balance shoe. Sometimes, you have to try both of these—the Egyptian bar shoe and the counter-balance shoe—to find out what works best on a given horse. If healing does not appear to be coming along with one shoe, try the other.

The counter-balance shoe is kind of an extra-long egg-bar, and I tilt it down to where it elevates the heel across the bar about 2 inches. There is more weight in the heel with this shoe, and the tendency is for the foot to land flat, rather than allowing the toe to break over, and thereby flex the tendon, which would interfere with healing.

Thrush

This is an infection that occurs around the frog and sole, and is all too common in horses who are kept in dirty pens or stalls. Thrush is characterized by its black discharge and foul smell. If left untreated, the entire frog can be eaten away by it. The best thing to do for thrush is to pare down the frog and sole, so it can be open and get some air. Promptly move the horse to clean surroundings, then treat the foot several times a day for 3 or 4 days, or until the condition clears up, with Coppertox (poured over the frog and sole). Clorox also works well for this.

Toed In

A horse who is toed in, or pigeon-toed, can be straightened out somewhat by lowering the inside of his front feet. Actually, this is not a real serious conformation problem when it comes to soundness. A horse who is toed in is not nearly as serious a problem as one who is toed out. With the toed-in horse, at least his weight is more centrally distributed over his feet, and that reason alone will help him stay

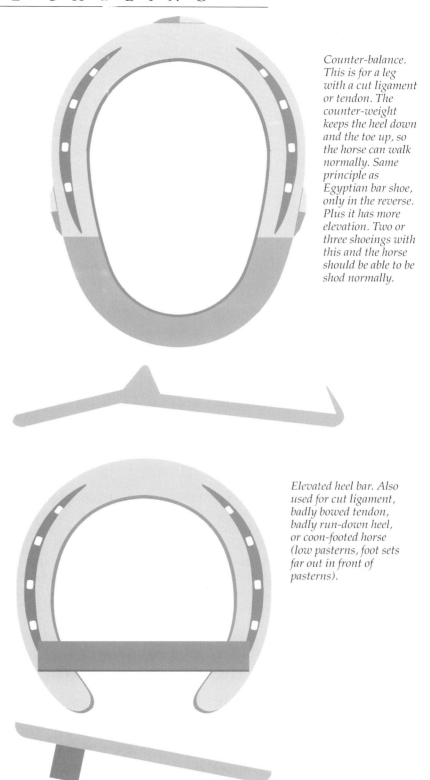

Counter-balance. This is for a leg with a cut ligament or tendon. The counter-weight keeps the heel down and the toe up, so the horse can walk normally. Same principle as Egyptian bar shoe, only in the reverse. Plus it has more elevation. Two or three shoeings with this and the horse should be able to be shod normally.

Elevated heel bar. Also used for cut ligament, badly bowed tendon, badly run-down heel, or coon-footed horse (low pasterns, foot sets far out in front of pasterns).

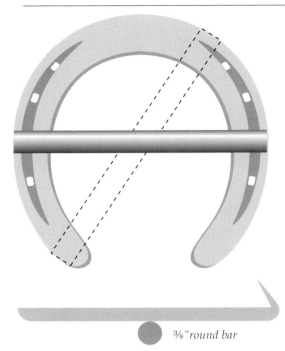

⅜"*round bar*

sound, even with hard work.

For extremely pigeon-toed horses, the pigeon-toed shoe (#11) is the ticket. The swelled heel goes outside of the hoof, the feathered heel inside, and with a rolled toe.

Toed Out

The problem with the toed-out horse is that he has a lot of extra stress on the inside of his feet, because of the way they are pointed. It is helpful to this horse to let him stand more squarely by doing the opposite in trimming his feet to what was done with a toed-in horse. In other words, we want to lower the outside of his feet. The winging/paddling shoe (#8) works well on toed-out horses.

Winging and Paddling

This goes along with being toed out. The horse's front feet wing outward with each step he takes. Use the winging/paddling shoe (#8) to help correct this.

Wire Cuts

Most wire-cut feet have a tendency to grow more hoof, faster, than feet that have not been injured in this manner. This is especially true if the cut or cuts were to the inside of the heel. In that case, the heel would probably outgrow the rest of the foot. For this type of cut, it is very important to work on keeping this heel trimmed down to a normal position. The tendency people have is to let the heel continue to grow, and to simply not take off the toe on that foot. The horse often stands more on his toe than on his heel with an injury like this, and that contributes to the excessive heel growth. The foot continues to grow out of proportion, and the resulting stress to it can cause bleeding around the coronet band.

The foot needs to be let down with each trimming and shoeing until it resumes a normal condition. Continue to rasp off any scarring on the hoof itself.

Some people try to keep a bar shoe on an injured foot like this, but I have found if I use an open shoe, it has a tendency to clean out more frequently than it would with a bar shoe, which tends to hold all the dirt and compaction in that area, which in turn contributes to the original problem. The excessive growth comes from a disruption in circulation to that area of the foot. A shoe that works well for horses who grow excessively high heels is the club-footed shoe (#2).

There is also a tendency for the foot to want to contract, but if we can keep the foot widened out by continually letting the heel down and shoeing with the open shoe, that problem can also be avoided. The contracted heel shoe (#5) is an option that might be used.

Generally, a cut on a hind foot will never cause the problem it will on a front foot, probably because the horse carries more weight on his front feet. Something else—keeping these cuts saturated with a wound salve and covered with a bell boot will keep them soft and protected from further injury.

Curative Burning

1/ *To prepare for the burning technique, the end of a rasp was heated in the forge, flattened out, and heated again.*

This type of treatment is used to put flexibility in a hoof that is frog- and sole-bound or otherwise restricted. For example, this type of treatment might help a club foot open up more, expanding into more of a normal, healthy-looking hoof. In the following photos, this procedure is used on a horse who was showing chronic lameness in both front feet.

The horse was diagnosed as having bursitis in the navicular area—in other words, pre-navicular. The horse was probably predisposed for this condition, having fairly straight pasterns. He had been shod previously with wedge pads, which raised his heels, but that seemed to make his lameness even worse. His left front foot was also somewhat of a club foot, and was noticeably smaller than his right front foot. He was also definitely frog- and sole-bound.

After both front feet were opened up with the burning technique, and he was shod with concave roller-motion shoes on both feet, he walked away sound and resumed his summer horse-show schedule. In the years that followed, this gelding did gradually develop navicular disease, but he maintained a fairly useful life, largely free of pain, through regular trimming and/or shoeing, and the occasional use of pads (sometimes wedge pads, sometimes not). The horse was shod according to "the change-up" principle mentioned in Chapter 5. Today, the horse is primarily retired and in his golden years. But he can still take a rider for a run across the pasture.

2/ *Burning around the perimeter of the frog helped open up the heel, allowing it to resume natural growth. The burning process does not strike any nerves unless the rasp is pressed too deep. When burning a hoof, simply move the rasp immediately if you feel any tenseness in the horse. I have never seen a horse blow up from this process; it seems to feel good to the horse.*

3/ *A fan pattern was also burned into the sole, again to allow expansion of growth in the area.*

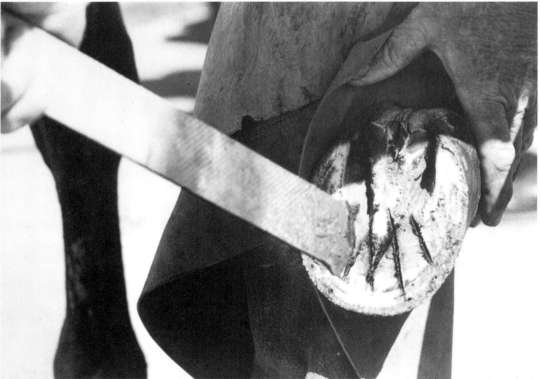

4/ A properly burned hoof.

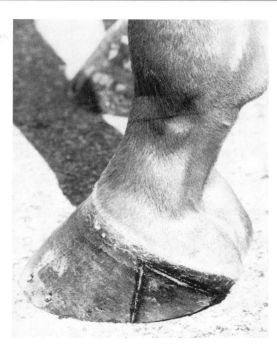

5/ A "7" was burnt into the hoof wall in this fashion on both sides of the hoof (both feet). This also adds flexibility to the heel area, which in turn lessens concussion and promotes healthy growth.

6/ Finally, the egg-shaped concave roller-motion shoe was put on both feet to help ease stress, or concussion, to the sole of the hoof.

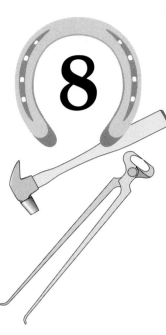

SPECIAL CONSIDERATION:
THE YOUNG & THE OLD HORSE, DRAFT, SHOW, & RETIRED RACE HORSE

8

Young Horse

WE TALKED ABOUT the importance of "trimming" foals' hoofs with a few careful strokes of the rasp in the chapter on basic trimming (how the foals' feet, front and back, nearly always need to be rasped slightly on the *outside* edge of each hoof to keep the foal developing with straight legs, rather than toeing out). And I told of

a method I like to use when handling foals for this type of work (the Short Rope Act) in the chapter on basic handling.

Here are some other special considerations the farrier should keep in mind when working with young horses, as well as another slightly different approach to handling colts and fillies when working on their feet.

Some of these babies will be relatively

Foals have a natural tendency to wear down the inside edges of their feet— because of their long legs and relatively short necks. This is why they invariably need to be lowered on the outside of their hoofs periodically during their first year, to keep their legs growing straight.

A farrier should work with any of his clientele who raise foals to ensure that the foals get off to a good start with their feet and legs.

weak right after they are born. Their pasterns will be low to the ground, they may be bow-legged or have some other leg problems. If a mare is giving plenty of milk, in just a few days her baby will straighten up in his legs and there really will not be too much to worry about. But, once in awhile, there will be one who is real bow-legged, or calf-kneed, or buck-kneed, or something, and this is the type who needs extra attention. Sometimes, the "baby toe" might not shed off of a foot, and it will just dry on the hoof and begin to create a ring there. If that happens, that baby toe needs to be gently rasped off for the hoof to grow normally.

I think it is important for a farrier to be willing to work with any of his clientele who raise foals—to look after the babies as well as the mares, ensuring that the foals get off to a good start with their feet and legs. An owner or farrier who puts in the time and effort to handle a foal early on will find it pays off later with having a more mature horse who is not only developing properly, but is good about having his feet trimmed. Folks who raise one or more foals are not necessarily knowledge-able or adept at handling them, so again, it is up to the farrier to be enough of a hand to catch these babies, work on them, and then show the owner how to work on them when the farrier is not around.

In about 5 minutes, one can have a foal caught and worked on, and at the same time show the owner how to catch the foal and work on his feet or doctor him or just get him used to being handled. Most colts who have a problem with their front or hind legs or feet need to be worked on every 3 or 4 weeks.

It helps to have one other person assist-ing the farrier when it comes to catching, haltering, and trimming foals or yearlings. Sometimes it works pretty well to ease a young horse like this between a fence or wall and a gate, then close the gate while the farrier reaches for the tail and twists it counter-clockwise to the side he is on. This will help immobilize the youngster while the other person reaches through the gate and slips a halter on him. Then the gate can be opened—but keep hold of the tail.

I can hold on to the tail, with it twisted just enough to keep the colt still, and then reach back and pick up a front foot or pick up a hind foot for trimming. Once the foot is between my legs, ready to be worked on, I can slowly release the tail-hold and the horse will continue to stand with the assistant holding on to the halter rope at the head. Twisting the tail like that is sort of like putting a twitch on the other end.

Ideally, I like to do a bunch of colts together in a big, safe box stall, preferably with walls (so a colt cannot rear up and get a leg caught over a rail). There might be six or eight colts in this big stall, and they will be jammed together in a corner with the two of us in there with them. I can slip up from behind, reach and catch a tail and twist it counter-clockwise, and hold one of the colts like this while the assistant quietly maneuvers up to put on a halter with a lead rope attached.

We will halter three or four of them like this, with the lead ropes hanging loose, then take them one at a time a little ways away from the others and work on their feet. There will be very little commotion in that stall, and the others will not be run-ning around.

If just one colt is put in a stall like this, it is pretty hard to get up to him to put that tail-hold on and halter him. Whenever a colt is separated like that, he will likely not want to be caught. A lot of times, if there is just one colt to do, I will get him in a stall and put the mare in with him, or if his momma is not there, put in a gentle horse. The baby will end up on the other side of that horse, and I can quietly reach around the horse and catch that baby's tail.

A word of caution: You cannot just run up to a colt and grab him by the tail and start twisting. He is liable to stand on his head and kick with both hind feet. Approach him from the side, so if he does kick, you are not directly behind him. Use your other hand, the one not holding the tail, to steady yourself and the baby by

Putting in time and effort to handle a foal early on will pay off later.

135

placing that hand on his hip, until you have a chance to pick up a foot and slowly release the tail while the assistant keeps him steady on the front end.

Young horses who get used to having their tail twisted like this before a foot is picked up will likely expect and accept this routine as they get older. In other words, a person may have to hold the tail and twist for a couple seconds while picking up a hind foot, then a front foot.

Teaching these young horses to stand quietly is one of the most important factors in shoeing horses. But, after a farrier or owner puts in the time to start a colt right, that horse will grow up to be easy to shoe.

Most of the colts who have a problem in the front or hind feet need to be worked on every 3 or 4 weeks. If the owner can work on these colts, the farrier can show him what to do and leave an old rasp, and let the owner rasp the toe or heel as needed, in between visits by the farrier. All that will have to be done, most of the time, will be to rasp off the outside edge of each foot, especially the front feet, because it is the insides of those hoofs that will wear off the most. Lowering the outside of these feet will keep his feet and legs growing straight, rather than toeing out.

Remember that one swipe of the coarse side of a rasp can take off a sixteenth to an eighth of an inch, so do not press down when rasping on a foal's foot—just float the rasp across, from the inside to the outside. If we need to lower the outside of the foot, it is easy to just run the rasp over the bottom of the foot, working from the middle of the foot outward, and two or three swipes is probably about all that will be necessary. More than that might result in rasping away too much of the hoof. You can hold a foot to the side, then drop it like a pendulum and see how straight it lands. One swipe of the rasp can move a foot from a half-inch to an inch when it comes to straightening it from toeing in or out. Use the coarse side to take off the right amount of hoof, then turn the rasp over and use the fine side to roll the edge of the foot, to keep it from chipping or cracking. You can probably do this with the fine side without even repositioning the foot out in front of you.

Most everything that needs to be done to a baby's feet can be done with the rasp, up till he is about a yearling. Maybe use the hoof knife sparingly to clean up the frog a little bit. Other than that, most of these youngsters simply need their feet lowered on the outsides, front and back.

Some foals may arrive buck-kneed, however, in which the knees pitch forward unnaturally, or they may be born calf-kneed, in which the knees bend backwards unnaturally. These babies need some extra attention to grow out of either of these conditions. A veterinarian should be consulted, and the recommendation might be a combination vitamin shot of A, D, and E over a period of time. The farrier can help these foals, as well.

A colt who is buck-kneed will stand on his heels. One would think the opposite would be true, but it is not. The toe winds up growing excessively, and in a matter of 4 or 5 weeks, it is stuck out in front, kind of like a horn, and needs to be rasped off. Do not touch the heel with the rasp whatsoever! By taking the toe off, we can get the foal's knee to where it will come back to where it belongs, and the excessive growth in the toe will stop.

On the other hand, if a colt is calf-kneed, he will be standing excessively on his toe. Again, this is the opposite of what one would imagine for this condition. On a baby like this, take the heel off to get these legs straightened out.

With a lot of foals like this—buck-kneed or calf-kneed—with just a little corrective rasping they will be correct on their feet by the time they are 3 to 6 months old. But it does take some watching and "culturing" of these feet to get them lined out to where they will grow properly.

If a young horse is still buck-kneed or calf-kneed by the time he is being started into training, I will alternately raise and lower the heels on his front feet. I will raise his heels for one shoeing by taking off some toe, and then lower his heels the next shoeing by leaving more toe. In this way, by changing the foot, the suspensories will stretch and often equal out the leg, eliminating the buck knee or calf knee. A word of caution: When taking off the toe, do not go to extremes and stand the horse up too straight—that could do more harm than good.

For the first shoeing, I recommend that

the young horse is shod behind and left barefoot on the front, when he is just being started into training. This minimizes the damage a colt might do to himself starting out, reaching across and bumping himself, causing a splint or some windpuffs in his front legs, the result of being out of position and moving awkwardly initially. The next time you shoe this horse, you can shoe him on all four feet, but be prepared to shoe a back foot first, then a front foot. If the front foot is shod first, the colt will probably act like he has never been shod before. If you start in back, then go to the front, there probably will not be any trouble.

I am against working the young horse on the longe line, before he is really broke. A young horse can run to the end of that 30- or 40-foot line, get pulled back, and hurt a shoulder or pull a tendon. And if a horse is being worked in a small circle, he can pick up some bad habits—like wing-ing with whichever foot is in the lead. After a horse is broke, and can handle himself well, I think it is fine to give him some of his exercise in this manner. Splint boots or leg wraps should be used every time when longeing a horse, for protec-tion, and it is a good idea to use this type of leg protection when riding a young horse, too.

Epiphysitis is something else to watch for in foals. This generally occurs when a foal is from 1 to several months old, and is characterized by buckling over in the ankles and knees. These joints will not stay locked in position, but will appear to be weak and wobbly. This condition is caused by an imbalance in feed—usually in a colt who has an abundance of milk from his mother, and is fed hay and grain that is too rich in protein for him. A veterinarian should be consulted in such a case, but the vet will probably recommend immediately cutting back on the rich feed—especially grain—that the foal is consuming.

Most foals with epiphysitis will grow excessive heel and wear the toe off on those feet that are affected—sometimes just the front, sometimes the hind feet, sometimes all four. So, it is a good idea to lower the heels on these feet, to help save the toes, and also to roll the toes. Rolling the toes and lowering the heels will help stabilize those feet. Such colts should not

be shod, however. The added weight of shoes on feet and legs that are already under excessive stress could result in injury. With a change in diet, colts with epiphysitis will generally out-grow it by the time they are 14 or 15 months old. The end result might be joints that are a little larger than normal.

Older Horses

Older horses, the kind who are family pets, kind of retired, and stand around a lot, grow excessive toe and not enough heel. These horses need to be let down in their toes, and with the help of the farrier, get to where they are standing into their feet again.

As a general rule, the toe on a horse like this has become thicker. Where it should be $3/8$ths of an inch thick (from white line to shell), it might have developed to where it is $3/4$ths of an inch thick. If that is the case, the toe can be cut back to about $3/8$ths. If the horse has been in a dry climate, however, that toe can be very hard to cut. Something that will make it easier to cut will be a spell of wet weather, or the horse can be kept in a wet, muddy corral a couple of days, and that will soften the hoof, too.

The farrier can then clean out the foot real good, taking out excessive sole, clean-ing up the frog, saving what heel there is, and then cutting the toe back. For a lot of these horses, I will encourage proper growth by shoeing with a $3/8$ths-inch wedge pad, packed with oakum, on his front feet. This elevates the foot and changes the circulation, causing it to grow more in the way it should.

Usually, after shoeing such a horse one time with the wedge pad, in about 10 or 12 weeks he has probably grown sufficient heel. When you take off the shoes at that time, the sole should be soft enough to pare out some more of that, and then take off some more toe. And the horse can probably just be trimmed and left bare-foot. By getting him to stand into his foot like this, he will be a lot more comfortable.

An old kids' horse. Such horses tend to grow excessive toe and not enough heel.

Draft horses on farms and ranches often do well with occasional trimming, rather than regular shoeing.

Many old horses have a history of founder. That will make the toe grow excessively, too. After using this procedure, the old foundered horse will be a lot more comfortable. Very seldom do we ever find back feet that have grown and gotten as out of shape and as uncontrolled in growth as the front ones do. The main reason for this is the fact that more weight bears on the front than the back. Neglecting the feet is a contributing cause.

Draft Horses

Draft horses who are worked on farms and ranches, for the most part, have not been shod, and have done well with occasional trimming. Horses used in icy conditions in winter can be sharp-shod for traction, and such horses used on pavement or in rough, rocky conditions will do well to have shoes, too.

Traditionally, in some parts of the country where draft horses were used for haying, these horses would work for maybe 10 days, then have 10 days off.

The steady work in the hay fields, perhaps coupled with a somewhat rocky pasture, would keep their feet worn off pretty good, to where with just a little trimming those feet would stay in good, hard condition. They would need the time off after a week or so because they would begin to get sore around the neck and shoulders from the horse collar. While they were resting, other horses would be used. It is a good thing most of those horses did not need anything more than trimming, because a lot of them would have been "bear-cats" to nail shoes on.

Back in the days before tractors replaced a lot of draft horses on farms and ranches, those horses who did need to be shod were usually shod in blacksmith shops. They had stocks and hobbles to where a horse could have his feet tied up or tied to the floor, whatever it took to get four shoes nailed on. Those stocks were equipped with things that cranked and swung and were probably scary-looking to a horse, but the end result was, like it or not, the horse got shod without injury to himself or the blacksmith.

Too bad the Short Rope Act was not around in those days, because this proce-

dure works just as well on big horses as it does on little horses, thus eliminating the need for all that restraint when shoeing a horse like this. You trim and shoe a big horse the same way you do a smaller horse.

Show Horses

Show horses fall basically into two groups—pleasure horses and performance horses. For horses bred and trained for pleasure classes, it is desirable for them to have a slow, low, level way of going, moving with little knee action. For performance horses used in other events, particularly fast-paced events like reining or roping, in which the horse's athletic ability is being shown, knee action is not relevant to the judge.

So, in shoeing a young pleasure horse, it is good to start this type of horse with about a 50- to 52-degree angle to his front feet, and to shoe him with the lightest shoes you can. Most of these 2- or 3-year-olds starting out as pleasure horses are soft-going horses to begin with, and very few of them are up right on their feet anyway.

When a horse like this gets "too much knee"—in other words shows more knee action than the owner desires—it is usually a result of growing excessive heel on the front feet. It is a good idea to determine if excessive heel is the cause of this. If this is not the cause, it sometimes helps such a horse to roll the toes on his front feet. Still, there are some horses who just will not travel according to the owners' or trainers' desires. A heavier shoe will not make the horse travel low and level, but will probably make him toss his knees even more. The desire for a light shoe has led many to shoe pleasure horses with aluminum shoes. I prefer the light steel shoe over the aluminum shoe because the aluminum shoe is so thick that it elevates these horses off the ground too much. There is more chance for mud and debris to pack in the bottom of those shoes, and that extra weight causes the pleasure horse to use himself even more than he would with just a thin, little steel shoe.

Draft horses are still very useful on many ranches. In snow country, they may be hooked to a sled and driven to a hay stack in the snowy meadow. There the hay is transferred from stack to sled, and then the hay is taken through the herd and scattered. In these conditions, draft horses often fare well if left barefoot.

And for that reason, just having a normal, natural foot is generally the best way to go on these young horses in training for pleasure competition.

Most horses who are inclined to be high-heeled are generally straight-shouldered horses, and there is hardly any way this type will win in pleasure classes. But this type of horse can do well in reining or roping, for example. For a horse who is in training for pleasure, and has the conformation necessary for traveling in this fashion, i.e. long, sloping pasterns, raising the heel in the hind feet just a little (not over 52 degrees), will make this horse a little snappier in his hocks, and therefore make him more appealing to the judge. If a horse has too much heel in his hind feet, however, the result will be a lack of driving power at the lope. He will therefore pull himself forward more with his front feet at this gait, and the result will be more motion in his knees, and his head will probably bob up and down, too.

Note: if a horse has a problem in his front feet, like lameness caused by navicular disease, and a wedge pad is called for to help relieve pain, it is wise to remember that the pad will act in the same fashion as that of excessive heel, and the result will be more knee action. The point is, do not expect the horse to travel in really smooth fashion if he has wedge pads on his front feet.

One final note on show horses—and this has to do with the introduction of sliding plates to the young reining horse prospect. When we go from a conventional shoe to a sliding plate on the hind feet, and lower the angle of those feet by four degrees (to about 46 degrees), that alone is a big change for a horse to get used to. The horse needs to be started out easy, till he gets to where he is comfortable with what has been done to him. By starting easy, I mean I put a ¾-inch slider on

Young reining horses should not be started in a regular, wide sliding plate—a shoe like that is "too slick" to start with. A reining horse needs to be brought along with a transitional shoe for a shoeing or two in order to gain the confidence to eventually slide like this horse.

for the first time (³/₄-inch-wide sliding plate). This size is not as "slick" as the wider plates, and the idea is for the horse to not scare himself when he is asked to stop. If you go to the 1-inch or 1¼-inch slider right off, you might scare the horse when he is asked to really stop good, and there is a good possibility that the horse will not want to stop hard and slide like that again.

Retired Race Horses

Horses who have been to the racetrack, and shod with the light racing plates generally have feet that are opened up pretty wide, and their heels are underslung. When we start putting the regular saddle horse shoes on a retired race horse, preparing him to move on to other jobs, it takes a few shoeings to get those feet built back to where that horse can be used on something besides soft turf. He needs to grow some heel and shell, and get some body back into those feet; the bars and

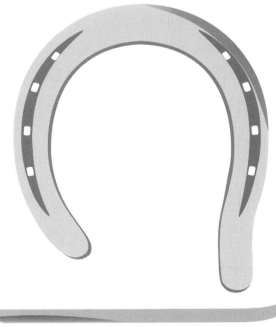

This shoe makes a good "beginning slider." The outside heel is a trailer, and the outside toe is rolled slightly.

Beginning slider.

141

A rim shoe is often used on performance horses, i.e. roping, barrel racing, polo—any sport where extra traction is desired. This type of shoe should be used on the front feet only. Rim shoes on the back feet are dangerous to the horse; they tend to make a horse over-reach and possibly injure a front leg or foot.

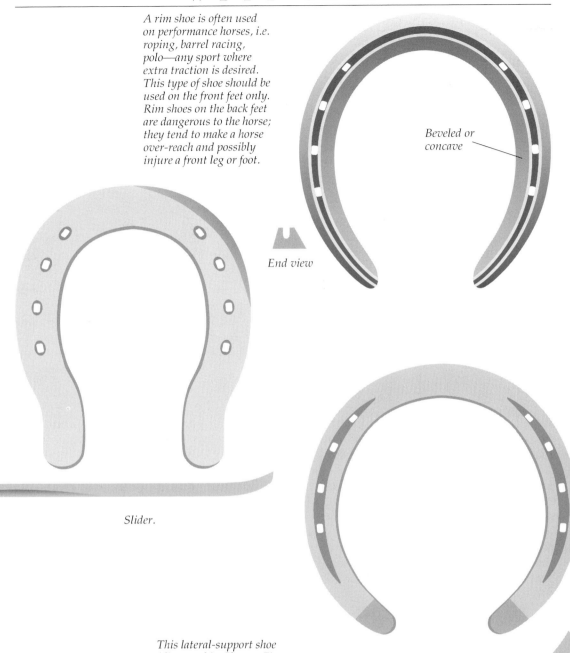

Beveled or concave

End view

Here is a handmade sliding plate. It may be of ¾-, 1-, or 1¼-inch-wide stock. There is no fullering, nail holes are counter-sunk, and if nail heads are sticking out of the holes slightly, they are rasped smooth, so as to not interfere with the sliding stops.

Slider.

This lateral-support shoe (discussed in Chapter 7) will often work well on a retired race horse who has underslung heels.

Lateral support shoe—race horses.

Through the years, a lot of Quarter Horses have gone from the racetrack to careers as timed-event horses in rodeo.

Photo by Tom Kimmel

frogs need strengthening. The back feet will often have excessive toe growth, and generally be grown to the outside real badly. At the race track, his feet have been cupped out, so that the soles are real thin, and he has been used to wearing the light racing plates.

Such a horse needs to be lowered on the outside of his feet, in back, and I generally put on squared-toe shoes on the back feet to keep him from over-reaching and knocking off the front shoes. This also helps the hock motion in such a horse—he will be standing more under himself. At the racetrack, he was probably running wide behind. His feet may also be about as wide as they are long, so it is real important, for that first normal shoeing, to put on shoes that are perhaps a size larger than he will wear the next time around, and then to fit those shoes so that you do not drive a nail into the white line.

I will use a 7- or 8-ounce shoe—heavier than what the horse was used to in the racing plates—and the horse will get along fine. The heavier shoe will help hold the foot together better, and thus keep it from spreading so much. If the horse's heels are run down, I will put the shoes in the fire and swell the heels on them, thus promoting heel growth and giving him some elevation. And I also like to fit the shoes wide enough around the heels so I can use heel nails, and not rely just on toe nails to hold the shoes on. It is also important that the shoes extend clear back to the bulbs of the horse's heels, for plenty of lateral support. It is a good idea to use concave shoes, because the horse will not be able to stand much sole pressure right away.

Very seldom does a customer with a racehorse go to a track close enough to where you can take care of the horse while he is racing. Trainers generally have a shoer who can take care of all their racehorses while they are running.

9

WELL-SHOD?

Some things to keep in mind regarding your horse's feet.

A HORSE OWNER who has read this far probably has a pretty good idea by now whether his shoer is doing a good job. There is a wide variety of materials ready-made to help the horseshoer correct hoof problems, and an expanding body of knowledge available to farriers, veterinarians, and laymen on hoof care, treatment of foot problems, and prevention of problems.

Here are some considerations to keep in mind when determining whether your horse's feet are being cared for properly.

How often is he shod?

Shoeing a horse too frequently is hard on his feet. Few horses can be shod every 30 days—they just do not get enough foot growth in that length of time. A horse grows about ½ inch of foot in about 6 weeks. Older horses will not grow as much hoof as younger horses, as a rule. Also, a horse's feet in dry weather will not grow as much as they will in moist weather.

An indication that a horse is being shod too frequently is being able to see the old nail holes in a hoof after the new shoes have been put on. I like to nearly cut off the entire nail pattern each time I do a horse—and I drive a higher nail than most people.

Another thing to watch for with nail holes: Holes too far forward in the hoof are a sure sign that the heel is not getting adequate support. The ideal is three nails placed on each side of the shoe, beginning with the holes closest to the heel, and leaving the fourth nail holes (those closest to the toe) without nails.

Remember the standing rasp.

We discussed this in the chapter on basic shoeing. It is a good rule-of-thumb test to see whether your horse has been trimmed and shod properly, and is in balance. Take a rasp (or ruler, or any comparable straight object) and place it perpendicular on the ground, right next to the heel of the shoe. The rasp should stand nearly straight up and down in line with the horse's cannon bone. A rasp that stands out in front of the cannon bone an

Remember the standing rasp--one test to help determine whether a horse has been shod properly. After shoeing, take a rasp or similar straight object and stand it up at the heel of the shoe. The rasp should come up alongside the cannon bone, either the middle of the bone or just touching the back of the bone. This tells you the horse's feet are in balance with his body.

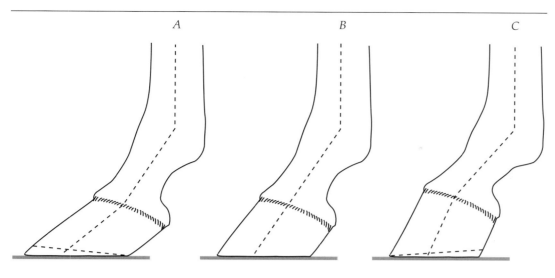

A   *B*   *C*

Check the angle of the feet after trimming. Illustration A shows a foot with too much toe left on (the dotted line at the bottom of the hoof shows where the trim should have been made). Illustration C shows a hoof with too much heel. And Illustration B shows a hoof that was trimmed about right.

inch or so means the foot had too much heel taken off and/or too much toe left on. This is a very common mistake beginning farriers make. Of course, if the rasp is standing behind the cannon bone, the foot is way out of balance the other direction.

Here's another little test to see if your horse is shod properly. Look at the old shoes pulled off. They should be uniform in size. In other words, the left and right front shoes should look the same, and the left and right hind shoes should look identical—and they should be worn evenly. There should be a little more worn off in the toe of each shoe, but other than that, the shoes should show even wear, from one side to the other.

Some beginning farriers will have a different size or shape of shoe on every foot. That is incorrect! As discussed earlier, if a horse has a problem with a club foot smaller than his other feet, that problem hoof needs to be cultivated and encouraged to grow and expand. It should not be restricted to a smaller shoe.

Pick those feet.

Horses' feet should be picked out regularly, especially if they are shod. Standing on a hard wad of mud all the time is not good. Unless a horse is in sand, he will get mud and rocks packed into his feet, packed in around the frogs and bars. This is what causes a lot of horses to become unsound, especially if they are prone to a navicular problem.

Horses used in an arena and kept stalled should have their feet picked out before being stalled each night. If a horse is kept outside, he still needs his feet picked out regularly if he is wearing shoes. Barefoot

horses get enough movement in their feet to prevent a buildup of mud. But a shoe prevents the foot from flexing enough to allow it to clean properly on its own.

I estimate that an additional 3 or 4 years can be added to a horse's useful life just by keeping his feet cleaned out. Picking out feet every day is a chore—but it also gets a horse more used to having his feet worked on, makes him better to handle, and easier for the farrier to work on.

A note on shavings.

A horse stalled in shavings can have drier hoofs than normal, especially if those shavings have a fairly high turpentine content, as some do. If that is the case, it is nearly a necessity to use some kind of hoof dressing to soften the feet.

Any of the soft woods make good shavings, and most shavings are from soft wood. By contrast, hard wood shavings can cause a horse to founder! So if a person runs across a "deal" in which he can get all the free shavings he wants from, say, a furniture manufacturer, he better know what kind of wood he is getting before using those shavings. Pine is a soft wood, and most shavings come from pine. Examples of hard woods to avoid include birch, walnut, oak, and cherry.

Straw bedding is used mainly in the East. Stalls are often cleaned, but not

145

This shoe is too big for any horse. It would be okay if the heels had been cut off at the dotted lines. Heels that are simply folded under on a shoe make it easy for the foot to pick up a rock and hold it in the crevice of the foot, in the frog and bar area, and the foot cannot shed it the way it should be able to.

Here is an example of a bad-fitting shoe. It is not symmetrical--one branch has been straightened too much, and then the heel was crudely cut off with bolt-cutters. The other branch looks fairly normal, but the heel was left too long.

stripped every day. Soiled straw is removed and fresh straw is laid down. The result is a good, soft, warm bed for the horse to stand and lay on, and the accumulation of moisture in the bedding tends to keep the feet in a soft condition.

However, one thing to watch for with straw bedding is thrush. Thrush will occur pretty easily as a result of the urine and moisture that builds up in the straw.

Hoof dressing.

Hoof dressing applied to the coronet band, on the hair, will melt from body heat and be absorbed through the hoof. This makes a dry hoof moist, and therefore more healthy and easier to trim and shoe. Such dressing is also very healing for bad sections in a hoof, like cracks, and again, the proper place to put it is on the coronet band.

Cracks.

Use caution when considering filling a crack in a hoof with some of the substances on the market today. Anything with lead is bad for a horse's system. Plastic wood is good to use—it has no toxicity—and some of the hoof repair kits on the market work well to fill a crack so it can be dressed off and look good.

A low-grade infection?

If your horse just does not seem to be doing well physically, and you cannot put your finger on the cause, he might be carrying a low-grade infection caused by bad nailing in one or more shoes. Remember that a common mistake beginning farriers make is not opening up a manufactured shoe adequately (especially a front shoe) so the nail holes are outside the white line of the hoof. If a shoe is too narrow for the foot, and a nail penetrates the white line, the horse may not show obvious signs of lameness, but can still be dragged down physically with a low-grade infection. He may appear a little bit listless and his hair coat may lose its natural luster.

Pads.

Thrush is a potential problem in horses' feet anytime pads are used. Oakum (a loose, stringy hemp fiber, treated with tar and used for a variety of purposes as a calking material) should always be used under the pad at the time of shoeing. It will help prevent moisture from getting between the pad and sole of the foot, and thereby helps prevent thrush from occurring. Plumber's oakum is the best to use under a pad.

I prefer to use leather pads, especially in summer, because plastic or neoprene pads can get pretty hot on feet. When I put on a full pad, I like to first dress the trimmed foot with pine tar or hoof dressing, then pack it with oakum as I apply the pad.

Silicone is used in place of oakum a lot—and I use it occasionally too. The problem to watch for with silicone is that it seems to seal the foot *too* much for the foot to stay healthy. If I use silicone one time, I don't use it the next. A sign that silicone is working against the foot will be seen in deterioration around the white line when the shoe and pad are removed.

Sometimes a horse with a sore-foot problem (like navicular disease) does not need full pads. Rim pads may give him adequate relief, instead, and these are better for the overall health of the feet. The main thing you have to do with rim pads is drill the heel of the shoes, and rivet the pad to the shoe so it does not crawl out from under the shoe during use.

I like to use a rim pad cut open about a half-inch wider to the inside, to cushion around the white line. This helps give the foot a little cushion, and perhaps keep the horse from being sore.

The main problem with a pad covering the foot: There is not much frog pressure. The foot cannot work properly if the frog is not being adequately stimulated to help aid circulation up through the leg. A horse can be ridden with pads at intervals to help him get over some soreness, but it would not be a good idea to have him shod with pads year-round.

Some show horses may need pads at the height of the show season because arenas get so hard. The frog gets bruised by the persistent pounding it takes.

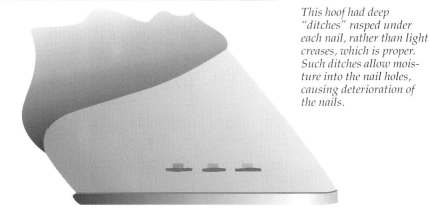

This hoof had deep "ditches" rasped under each nail, rather than light creases, which is proper. Such ditches allow moisture into the nail holes, causing deterioration of the nails.

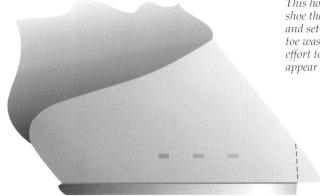

This hoof was shod with a shoe that was too short, and set too far back. The toe was "dubbed off" in an effort to make the foot appear more normal.

Snowy weather.

Snowballs can build up in a horse's feet if he stays shod during snowy weather. These balls of ice are bad because the horse no longer has flat footing. Riding him can be dangerous. He might also rock over and sprain an ankle, and if he is led inside on a concrete floor, he probably won't be able to stand.

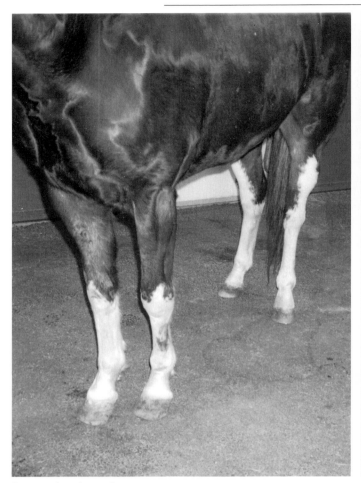 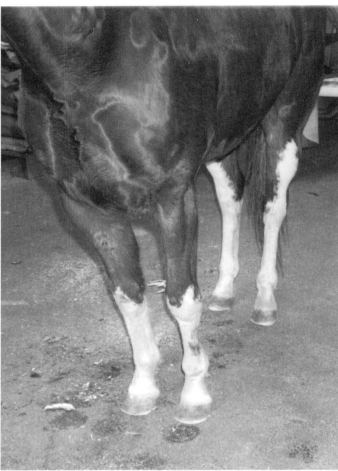

Proper trimming and shoeing enhance a horse's appearance as well as his performance. Compare this horse's feet and legs before he was trimmed (left) and immediately after trimming.

The easiest way to get snowballs out of the feet is to bump the shoe with a hammer. Usually, all that frozen packing will then fall out.

A horse who stands around on snowballs for an extended period of time will also likely get some freezing in his feet. This result may be a frozen area that looks like a bruise or even founder. These areas can be pretty sore, and sometimes you have to treat them as you would bruises on the sole. They can be pared out, unless they are really deep. In that case, the horse will probably be pretty sore, and may even require pads to help him get over the condition.

Very seldom do we see a problem with snowballs in a barefoot horse. So taking the shoes off in the wintertime, when there is snow on the ground, is a good idea if the horse is not being used. For a horse being ridden in snowy conditions, there is a snowball pad on the market that works pretty well. This pad has a rounded area in the middle of it that works up and down as the horse moves, and it pushes the snow out of the foot. It's available from farrier supply stores.

There are also a few shoes on the market that have a real good beveled inside edge. They work fairly well on horses being used in snow, mud, and ice. Most of the training plates, polo plates, and a lot of rim shoes have good beveled inside edges that work well to clean out snow and mud.

To pull a shoe.

It is not uncommon for a horse to get a loose shoe, or to pull just the heel of a shoe loose, and then bend the shoe. When that happens, the horse is walking around with the heel of that foot elevated anywhere from ⅜ to ½ inch. That will cause soreness. It is even worse if the horse is worked with a shoe in that condition.

If you cannot get a farrier to come right away and remove a loose or bent shoe, remove the shoe yourself and wait for the horse to be shod again before working him. If a horse loses a shoe on a trail, he can be ridden home if the distance is not too great or the trail is not too rocky. An Easy Boot carried in a saddlebag is a temporary fix, but a shoe that is bent still needs to be pulled first.

Pulling a loose shoe.

A variety of tools can be used to pull a shoe. Be creative—you need a hammer, or something to act as a hammer, and a blunt object to use with the hammer. The object is to first drive the clinches upward, or, if you have a rasp or file, you can file them off. With the clinches released, the nails can easily be pulled straight through the hoof as the shoe is removed.

For example, you might use a wood

chisel and a regular carpenter's hammer to straighten out the clinches by placing the chisel under a clinch and tapping the chisel on the handle to straighten the clinch.

After all the clinches are released, you could place the chisel at an angle on the outside edge of the shoe, and strike it with the hammer again to loosen the shoe and drive it off the hoof. Driving the shoe off in this manner is probably the best procedure for the layman. But you could also do a little prying with a crescent wrench, working the edge of the wrench under the shoe and tapping the handle with a hammer or something used as a hammer. A tire iron will also work well for this. The main idea is to release the clinches, then work the shoe off.

I do not file off or bend the clinches up when I prepare to remove a shoe with pull-off tongs, but I have the right tool and the right feel for using it without taking that initial step. However, the layman, improvising with other tools, will find that removing a shoe is easier if the clinches are dealt with first.

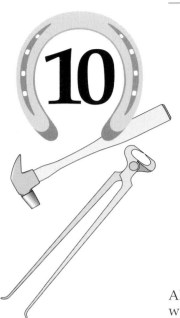

10

THE FARRIER-CLIENT RELATIONSHIP

The farrier should treat his horseshoeing as a business. The client should be considerate of the farrier's needs and schedule.

ANY HORSESHOER should be happy when he builds up a clientele that enables him to stay busy throughout the year. And any horse owner should be happy when he gets a good, reliable horseshoer he can count on to keep his horse well-shod. Unfortunately, the farrier-client relationship often leaves a lot to be desired.

Probably the biggest complaint clients have about horseshoers in general is,

"They hardly ever show up on time. Sometimes they don't show up, period!"

To farriers trying to get established, I advise you to treat horseshoeing as a business, beginning with the common courtesy of making and keeping appointments. There are valid reasons for being late to an appointment, but there is hardly ever an excuse for not phoning ahead to tell someone you are running behind schedule. Most horse

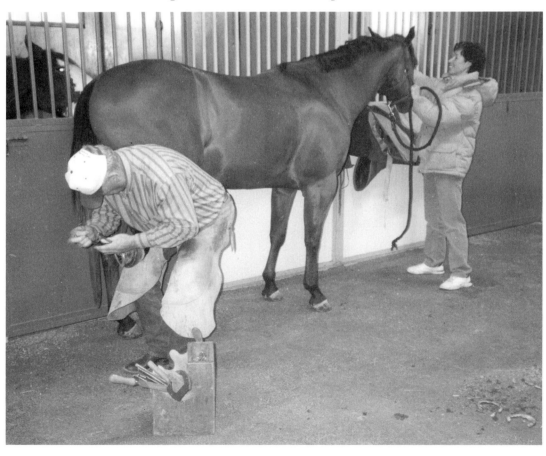

Shoeing a horse for one of my customers, Margaret Hammond.

A state fair horse show in progress. A farrier can acquire a lot of new business by making himself available during such events.

owners want to be home when the farrier shows up to do the work, and most have jobs and other things that need attention, as well. Waiting around for the horseshoer to pull up the driveway long after he is due is an aggravation.

To the client, I recommend calling the farrier at least a week or 10 days ahead of time, making an appointment with him. Of course, if there is an emergency, a shoe comes off or something, then by all means call the farrier and expect him to make room in his schedule to take care of the problem. This is one reason a horseshoer might be running late on a particular day.

He might also find himself in a time crunch when a client requests that he also trim or shoe additional horses, who were not scheduled to be worked on that day. I think the horseshoer should go ahead and do those horses—the owner obviously needs them done, or he would not have led them out. But the farrier needs to let his other clients know that his schedule has been changed. A lot of times it works well for the client with the extra horses to make any necessary phone calls.

It also helps a farrier to stay on schedule if an owner has his horses caught, rather than having to walk out in a pasture to get them.

Keep in mind, too, that a horse who has been worked recently is generally easier to shoe than a fresh horse who has not had exercise. Even if the horse was worked the day before the shoer arrives, he will likely stand more quietly than one who has not had any work. A person with a horse who is fidgety and will not stand quietly can often give that horse 10 to 15 minutes of exercise, maybe on a walker or by running him around a round pen, and see a big change in attitude.

Remember also that holding a horse correctly while the shoer works on him encourages good behavior in the horse. Use a good heavy halter the horse can feel, and give him at least a foot of slack in the lead rope, so he can relax a bit, rather than trying to put his head in a "vise-grip" with your hands on his halter.

Stand on the same side of the horse the farrier is working on. That way, if the horse suddenly spooks at something, he will likely jump away from both the handler and farrier, rather than on top of one or the other.

Flies can be a problem during shoeing. Some horses can stand flies better than others, but if flies are bothering a horse being shod, and seem to be making him move around, swish his tail excessively, and want to constantly take his foot away from the farrier, it sure does help to have some fly spray on hand. Most flies are an irritation to a horse, but some of the big horse flies or bees, those that can really bite and sting, can cause a horse to react in such a way that the horseshoer working on a foot can get injured.

Both the shoer and owner should be aware of any other circumstances that would cause a normally quiet, well-mannered horse to become fretful. Shoeing next to a pen of active horses would likely cause the horse getting shod to want to join in on the activity. Shoeing at feeding time for the horse can also make him fretful. Dogs underfoot, children on bicycles nearby, or a chatty bystander might be other "reasons" a particular horse might not stand still for shoeing.

The subject of dogs needs comment. I believe if a horseshoer insists on taking his dog with him to his appointments, he should at least leave the dog in the pickup. Better yet, leave the dog at home. People are paying to have their horses shod, not have their property "marked" by the horseshoer's dog.

On the other hand, I feel the owner's dog has a perfect right to be around, if that is what the owner wants, and the dog doesn't create problems with the horse being worked on. I do have to draw the line, however, when the owner's dog becomes overly interested in my toolbox.

Customer service is important in any vocation. That is why a farrier who wants to build his client base is well-advised to work on weekends. That is when most people are home, and that is when most want the work done. I have received a lot of steady work through the years from folks who had been put off by their previous shoer over a weekend scheduling conflict. A farrier can take off a couple of days in the middle of the week, and rest then. After his business is better established, then he may be able to gradually arrange his personal schedule so he gets more weekends off.

To the horse owner: Please pay your horseshoer promptly, as soon as he has completed the work. If the tables were turned, this might be the biggest complaint horseshoers have about their clientele.

Finally, horse owners should not hesitate to ask questions of their shoer in regards to their horses' feet and way of going. If an owner suspects a problem, maybe detects a slight lameness or some change in gait, it is a good idea to alert the shoer to this. By the same token, the shoer should make a careful evaluation of the horse, as far as his feet and way of going are concerned, and also speak up with advice when he sees something unsafe for the horse.

A lot of new horse owners need all the help they can get when it comes to proper safety around horses and care of their horses. If a piece of equipment, a section of fence or a gate, is obviously a wreck waiting to happen, please do the horse and his owner a favor by diplomatically pointing out the problem and offering an alternative. A horse may be obviously too skinny or too fat, or may have a tank of foul water that needs to be changed. Folks new to the horse business need these things explained to them. That is why, as I said earlier in this book, a horseshoer needs to be enough of a horse hand to help owners, to a certain degree, care for and handle their horses.

Here are some examples of equine health problems the farrier is likely to notice, from time to time, which the owner may not recognize.

• A horse may have some raw, abrasion-like areas around his hocks. It looks like he may have rubbed himself that way, while lying down and getting up. But the cause can be chicken mites. These parasites can be carried by birds, even if a chicken is not within miles of the horse. Topical treatments are available at places like feed stores or veterinarian hospitals.

• Sometimes, a farrier sees that a horse seems extra silly around his head, especially his ears. The horse may start shaking his head and lay down an ear. Nine times out of ten, a close inspection will reveal the horse's ears are filled with ticks.

• While working on a horse, I might notice some bumps on his back. They might be grubs, and he should not be ridden until the grubs are removed.

• Or a horse with a watery eye—it might be an indication of a clogged tear duct. In these cases, I point out the problem, and recommend the owner call a veterinarian for treatment.

PROFILE: DON BASKINS

Don Baskins.

DON BASKINS took an early interest in horseshoeing. He remembers, at age 4, living with his family on the Wyoming Hereford Ranch near Cheyenne and watching the ranch horses being shod.

"Horseshoers from Fort Francis E. Warren, there at Cheyenne, would come out to the ranch to do the horses, and I would watch them go about their work," Don says. "That's when I first started figuring I wanted to be a horseshoer."

Don was born in 1931, the youngest of two boys in the John and Dorothy Baskins family. Dorothy was the ranch cook, and John was foreman of the main ranch for several years. When Don was 7, the family moved to another part of the ranching operation, the Campstool Ranch east of Cheyenne near Carpenter, Wyoming. Dad was general manager of the outfit, and Don attended grade school about 15 miles from home.

Don remembers that the Campstool Ranch kept a government Remount stallion, and raised horses and mules. And his grandfather, W.C. Vandever, who

ranched at Kim, Colo., also raised Remount horses and mules, and was something of a gypsy horse trader, as well. Don recalls traveling with his grandfather for weeks at a time, with team and wagon, trading for horses and bringing them back to the ranch. These are the things that stick in his mind—ranches with horses and men who could "do something" with them.

"I always seemed to get myself situated to where I could observe good horse people," he says. "I always had older friends, never kids my own age. I was generally attracted to some old fellow I thought could do something. Men like that would usually take time to teach a kid something, too, if the youngster showed he was trying to learn.

"There was one old man at Cheyenne named Earl Vandehigh, who had a place north of town where he raised polo ponies and Thoroughbred running horses. At the age of 5 and 6, I was a 'big friend' of his."

Don got a job breaking colts for Eddie McCarty, near Chugwater, Wyo., when he was 12. This was the McCarty of McCarty and Elliott rodeo fame—premier bucking horse breeders.

"After a while," Don laughs, "I figured out that those colts I was working with were all out of a bunch of old bucking mares. But it was good experience, and I got in on trailing horses to some of the rodeos that summer."

He was already shoeing horses by then too.

"I shod horses for Henry Peterson, a friend of my folks, who raced chuck wagons in Canada," Don continued, "and I spent time on the old Circle Bar Ranch at West Plains, Colo. (near Sterling), when I spent a winter with my Uncle Carl, my mother's brother, who worked on the ranch. I went to school at West Plains, and the best part of that was getting to know the horsemen in the area—men like Marshall Peavy and Jack Casement."

The area was (and still is) home to the Anderson ranch and rodeo family. The Earl Anderson Memorial Rodeo is still held every June, over Father's Day weekend, at Grover, Colorado. Don got his start as a rodeo clown and bullfighter at the Grover rodeo. His rodeo career was fun while it lasted, but Don's main interest was still horseshoeing.

He went to high school at Campion Academy near Loveland, Colorado. Don was big for his age—and strong—and that may have helped him land a job at the school. "I rode in there horseback and went to work as assistant to the dean and got 20 cents an hour," he remembers. "My job was to work in the dormitory, where I helped take care of all the other kids. It was a boarding school, a lot of children came from out of state, and some had come from problem homes.

"But we straightened out most of 'em there."

One of Don's main assignments was ensuring that everyone attended class and various other school functions. "I'd have to gather anyone who was missing. Might have to look under a mattress or in a closet or behind a tree, but I'd always get 'em gathered, and we kept perfect attendance."

Don studied other horseshoers at work, as time went by. These were older men, people he figured knew more than he did—and he studied the old cavalry and other horseshoeing manuals. "Nearly all the new shoes that have been introduced in modern times were in use in the 1800s," he says. "They're nearly all pictured somewhere in one or more old books. Through the years, things have been rediscovered, but there is not a lot that is really new."

Don served in the United States Marine Corps from 1952 to 1955. His talent as a horseshoer was quickly recognized, and as a result he spent his military career shoeing horses.

"I was stationed at El Toro, Calif., in a special service unit," he explains. "We sent some horses to Korea from there, but we also had a riding stable for the officers' wives."

After his discharge from the Marines, Don remained in California till 1960, shoeing a variety of gaited horses, harness and show ponies—"and that's when I perfected my fire work (at the forge)," he says.

Don settled in New Mexico in 1960. He liked the country, and liked the fact it was kind of in the middle of a five-state area in which he wanted to work. He and his wife, Oda, settled in Tucumcari and raised a son and two daughters. Don is proud of his family. Oda has been his biggest supporter, and still serves as telephone receptionist and travel/itinerary agent for his horseshoeing business. Their son, John Bradley, is a computer expert and chemical engineer in Dallas; oldest daughter, Cara Dawn, is a restaurant manager in Albuquerque; and younger daughter, Sarah Beth, a former Miss New Mexico Teen U.S.A., is an intensive care nurse in a hospital cardiac unit in Lubbock, Texas.

"I think I'm a born gypsy horseshoer, at heart," Don says. "Remember, my grandfather had those tendencies. I often think it would have been nice to travel the country, shoeing as I went, never shoeing the same horse twice."

In the early years, when Don was still building his business, he and Oda, with baby in arms, did a fair amount of traveling with a car and trailer in tow. The trailer had a sign that read: "Don Baskins—Horseshoeing—No Phone, No Home."

Don thought it was a great joke, and enjoyed the reactions of strangers who looked at the sign and then looked at the little wife and child. "Oda never saw the humor in that sign," Don says.

Don is slowing down a bit these days, but he still drives to a lot of customers in some far-flung places. And in recent years he even started flying regularly to Phoenix, to do some corrective shoeing there.

"I think I'll always have to do some shoeing," he says. "I've known some old fellows who got up in their 80s and could still shoe a horse. I think I'm one of those people.

"Besides," he added, "I'll probably live to be 90 or 100 just to aggravate people."

—Randy Witte

INDEX

SHOE INDEX

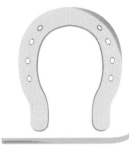

Normal flat shoe—best all-around shoe to use. Page 100.

Half-round shoe—good pleasure riding shoe; also helps a horse who tends to stumble. Page 68, 100.

Rim shoe—a high performance shoe (roping, barrel racing, polo, etc.). Use on front feet only. Page 142.

Beginning slider for young reining horses. Use on back feet for one or two shoeings before graduating to regular slider; trailer goes to outside. Page 141.

Slider (or sliding plate) for reining horses. Page 142.

A rolled toe on a shoe enables the foot to break over more quickly. This often helps a horse with early navicular disease, or a horse who tends to stumble.

Concave roller-motion shoe—often effective on founder, navicular, ringbone, sidebone. Use with side clips. Page 110.

Another view of the concave roller-motion shoe, this one with the necessary side clips. Page 110.

Concave roller-motion shoe with swelled heels—good for use on shelly feet and/or low heels. Page 112.

A toe clip can help secure the shoe on a shelly foot, preventing the shoe from sliding back by relieving stress on the nails.

Club-footed shoe. Page 110.

Calked ankle on a shoe for a bow-legged horse. Page 110.

Cow-hocked shoe—helps straighten the hocks. Page 111.

Contracted heel shoe. Page 111.

Spoon bar shoe—good for founder and chronic navicular disease. Page 111.

Winging and paddling shoe. Page 112.

Loose-hocked shoe—stabilizes limber hocks. Page 112.

Bog spavin shoe. Page 113.

Pigeon-toed shoe. Page 113.

Egg-shaped bar shoe—for bruised bulbs, broken bars, weak heels, underslung heels. Page 113.

Tapered heel calks—for extra traction. Page 102.

Toe bar with heel calks—for extra traction. Page 103.

Screw-in calks—for extra traction. Page 102.

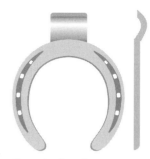

Egyptian bar shoe—for severed tendon. Page 128, 129.

Counter-balance shoe—for severed tendon. Page 128, 129.

Elevated heel bar—for cut ligament, badly bowed tendon, rundown heel. Page 129.

Wood shingle slipped under a pad can help a horse who is trying to survive initial founder. Page 118, 119.

Bowed rocker—a regular shoe with rolled toe and heel, used on a horse that has previously foundered. Page 118.

Full pad—can be used to protect sore sole, frog, heel. Such pads may have a wedge over the heel to elevate that area, possibly aiding navicular, foundered, or stifled horse. Page 103.

Open wedge pad—offers nearly the same protection as a full pad, but the openess allows for more natural growth and function of the foot. Page 103.

Toe pad. This shows an open wedge pad that has been turned around to provide elevation in the toe—used on a horse who had too much toe removed by an inexperienced farrier during a recent trimming. The horse will be able to function while the toe grows back.

Side-weight shoe—to counteract severe winging, paddling. Page 101.

Toe-weight shoe—to counteract excessive knee action. Page 101.

Heel-weight shoe—to counteract excessive extension. Page 101.

Lateral support shoe—for dropped or rundown heels. Page 121, 142.

Stifle shoe. Page 127.

Memphis bar shoe—for ringbone. Page 130.

Books Published by
WESTERN HORSEMAN®

ARABIAN LEGENDS by Marian K. Carpenter
280 pages and 319 photographs. Abu Farwa, *Aladdinn, *Ansata Ibn Halima, *Bask, Bay-Abi, Bay El Bey, Bint Sahara, Fadjur, Ferzon, Indraff, Khemosabi, *Morafic, *Muscat, *Naborr, *Padron, *Raffles, *Raseyn, *Sakr, Samtyr, *Sanacht, *Serafix, Skorage, *Witez II, Xenophonn.

BACON & BEANS, by Stella Hughes
144 pages and 200 -plus recipes for delicious western chow.

BARREL RACING, Completely Revised by Sharon Camarillo
128 pages, 158 photographs and 17 illustrations. Teaches foundation horsemanship and barrel racing skills for horse and rider, with additional tips on feeding, hauling and winning.

CALF ROPING by Roy Cooper
144 pages and 280 photographs. Complete coverage of roping and tying.

CHARMAYNE JAMES ON BARREL RACING
by Charmayne James with Cheryl Magoteaux
192 pages and over 200 color photograps. Charmayne shares the training techniques and philosophy that made her the most successful barrel racer in history. Also included are vignettes of horses and riders that illustrate Charmayne's approach to indentifying and correcting problems in barrel racing, as well as examples and experiences from over 20 years as a world-class competitor in this exciting event.

COWBOYS & BUCKAROOS by Tim O'Byrne
176 pages and over 250 color photograps. The author, who's spent 20 years on ranches and feedyards, explains in great detail the trade secrets and working lifestyle of this North American icon. Readers can follow the cowboy crew through the four seasons of a cattle-industry year, learn their lingo and the Cowboy Code they live by, understand how they start colts, handle cattle, make long circles in rough terrain and much, much more. Many interesting sidebars, including excerpts from the author's personal journal offering firsthand accounts of the cowboy way.

CUTTING by Leon Harrel
144 pages and 200 photographs. Complete guide to this popular sport.

FIRST HORSE by Fran Devereux Smith
176 pages, 160 black-and-white photos, numerous illustrations. Step-by-step information for the first-time horse owner and/or novice rider.

HELPFUL HINTS FOR HORSEMEN
128 pages and 325 photographs and illustrations. WH readers and editors provide tips on every facet of life with horses and horse owners share. Chapters include: Equine Health Care; Saddles; Bits and Bridles; Gear; Knots; Trailers/Hauling Horses; Trail Riding/Backcountry Camping; Barn Equipment; Watering Systems; Pasture, Corral and Arena Equipment; Fencing and Gates; Odds and Ends.

IMPRINT TRAINING by Robert M. Miller, D.V.M.
144 pages and 250 photographs. Learn to "program" newborn foals.

LEGENDS 1 by Diane Ciarloni
168 pages and 214 photographs. Barbra B, Bert, Chicaro Bill, Cowboy P-12, Depth Charge (TB), Doc Bar, Go Man Go, Hard Twist, Hollywood Gold, Joe Hancock, Joe Reed P-3, Joe Reed II, King P-234, King Fritz, Leo, Peppy, Plaudit, Poco Bueno, Poco Tivio, Queenie, Quick M Silver, Shue Fly, Star Duster, Three Bars (TB), Top Deck (TB) and Wimpy P-1.

LEGENDS 2 by Jim Goodhue, Frank Holmes, Phil Livingston, Diane Ciarloni
192 pages and 224 photographs. Clabber, Driftwood, Easy Jet, Grey Badger II, Jessie James, Jet Deck, Joe Bailey P-4 (Gonzales), Joe Bailey (Weatherford), King's Pistol, Lena's Bar, Lightning Bar, Lucky Blanton, Midnight, Midnight Jr, Moon Deck, My Texas Dandy, Oklahoma Star, Oklahoma Star Jr., Peter McCue, Rocket Bar (TB), Skipper W, Sugar Bars and Traveler.

LEGENDS 3 by Jim Goodhue, Frank Holmes, Diane Ciarloni, Kim Guenther, Larry Thornton, Betsy Lynch
208 pages and 196 photographs. Flying Bob, Hollywood Jac 86, Jackstraw (TB), Maddon's Bright Eyes, Mr Gun Smoke, Old Sorrel, Piggin String (TB), Poco Lena, Poco Pine, Poco Dell, Question Mark, Quo Vadis, Royal King, Showdown, Steel Dust and Two Eyed Jack.

LEGENDS 4
216 pages and 216 photographs. Several authors chronicle the great Quarter Horses Zantanon, Ed Echols, Zan Parr Bar, Blondy's Dude, Diamonds Sparkle, Woven Web/Miss Princess, Miss Bank, Rebel Cause, Tonto Bars Hank, Harlan, Lady Bug's Moon, Dash For Cash, Vandy, Impressive, Fillinic, Zippo Pine Bar and Doc O' Lena.

LEGENDS 5 by Frank Holmes, Ty Wyant, Alan Gold, Sally Harrison
248 pages, including about 300 photographs. The stories of Little Joe, Joe Moore, Monita, Bill Cody, Joe Cody, Topsail Cody, Pretty Buck, Pat Star Jr., Skipa Star, Hank H, Chubby, Bartender, Leo San, Custus Rastus (TB), Jaguar, Jackie Bee, Chicado V and Mr Bar None.

LEGENDS 6 by Frank Holmes, Patricia Campbell, Sally Harrison, GloryAnn Kurtz, Cheryl Magoteaux, Heidi Nyland, Bev Pechan, Juli S. Thorson
236 pages, including about 270 photographs. The stories of Paul A, Croton Oil, Okie Leo Flit Bar, Billietta, Coy's Bonanza, Major Bonanza, Doc Quixote, Doc's Prescription, Jewels Leo Bar, Colonel Freckles, Freckles Playboy, Peppy San, Mr San Peppy, Great Pine, The Invester, Speedy Glow, Conclusive, Dynamic Deluxe and Caseys Charm

NATURAL HORSE-MAN-SHIP by Pat Parelli
224 pages and 275 photographs. Parelli's six keys to a natural horse-human relationship.

PROBLEM-SOLVING, Volume 1 by Marty Marten
248 pages and over 250 photos and illustrations. Develop a willing partnership between horse and human — trailer-loading, hard-to-catch, barn-sour, spooking, water-crossing, herdbound and pull-back problems.

PROBLEM-SOLVING, Volume 2 by Marty Marten
A continuation of Volume 1. Ten chapters with illustrations and photos.

RAISE YOUR HAND IF YOU LOVE HORSES by Pat Parelli w. Kathy Swan
224 pages and over 200 black and white and color photos. The autobiography of the world's foremost proponent of natural horsemanship. Chapters contain hundreds of Pat Parelli stories, from the clinician's earliest remembrances to the fabulous experiences and opportunities he has enjoyed in the last decade. As a bonus, there are anecdotes in which Pat's friends tell stories about him.

RANCH HORSEMANSHIP by Curt Pate w. Fran Devereux Smith
220 pages and over 250 full color photos and illustrations. Learn how almost any rider at almost any level of expertise can adapt ranch-horse-training techniques to help his mount become a safer more enjoyable ride. Curt's ideas help prepare rider and horse for whatever they might encounter in the round pen, arena, pasture and beyond.

REINING, Completely Revised by Al Dunning
216 pages and over 300 photographs. Complete how-to training for this exciting event.

RIDE SMART, by Craig Cameron w. Kathy Swan
224 pages and over 250 black and white and color photos. Under one title, Craig Cameron combines a look at horses as a species and how to develop a positive, partnering relationship with them, along with good, solid horsemanship skills that suit both novice and experienced riders. Topics include ground-handling techniques, hobble-breaking methods, colt-starting, high performance maneuvers and trailer-loading. Interesting sidebars, such as trouble-shooting tips and personal anecdotes about Cameron's life, complement the main text.

RODEO LEGENDS by Gavin Ehringer
Photos and life stories fill 216 pages. Included are: Joe Alexander, Jake Barnes & Clay O'Brien Cooper, Joe Beaver, Leo Camarillo, Roy Cooper, Tom Ferguson, Bruce Ford, Marvin Garrett, Don Gay, Tuff Hedeman, Charmayne James, Bill Linderman, Larry Mahan, Ty Murray, Dean Oliver, Jim Shoulders, Casey Tibbs, Harry Tompkins and Fred Whitfield.

ROOFS AND RAILS by Gavin Ehringer
144 pages, 128 black-and-white photographs plus drawings, charts and floor plans. How to plan and build your ideal horse facility.

STARTING COLTS by Mike Kevil
168 pages and 400 photographs. Step-by-step process in starting colts.

THE HANK WIESCAMP STORY by Frank Holmes
208 pages and over 260 photographs. The biography of the legendary breeder of Quarter Horses, Appaloosas and Paints.

TEAM PENNING by Phil Livingston
144 pages and 200 photographs. How to compete in this popular family sport.

TEAM ROPING WITH JAKE AND CLAY by Fran Devereux Smith
224 pages and over 200 photographs and illustrations. Learn about fast times from champions Jake Barnes and Clay O'Brien Cooper. Solid information about handling a rope, roping dummies and heading and heeling for practice and in competition. Also sound advice about rope horses, roping steers, gear and mounting.

TRAIL RIDING by Janine M. Wilder
128 pages and over 150 color photographs. The author, who's ridden in all 48 states, Hawaii and the Yucatan over the last 20 years, has compiled a comprehensive guide that covers all the bases a trail rider needs in this fast-growing sport. She offers proven methods for developing a solid trail horse, safe ways to handle a variety of terrain, solutions for common trail problems, plus tips and resources on how to travel with horses. Interesting sidebars document her experiences on the trail.

WELL-SHOD by Don Baskins
160 pages, 300 black-and-white photos and illustrations. A horse-shoeing guide for owners and farriers. Easy-to-read, step-by-step how to trim and shoe a horse for a variety of uses. Special attention is paid to corrective shoeing for horses with various foot and leg problems.

WESTERN TRAINING by Jack Brainard
With Peter Phinny. 136 pages. Stresses the foundation for western training.

WIN WITH BOB AVILA by Juli S. Thorson
Hardbound, 128 full-color pages. Learn the traits that separate horse-world achievers from also-rans. World champion horseman Bob Avila shares his philosophies on succeeding as a competitor, breeder and trainer.

Western Horseman, established in 1936, is the world's leading horse publication. For subscription information: 800-877-5278
To order other Western Horseman books: 800-874-6774 • Western Horseman, PO Box 470725, Fort Worth, TX 76147
Web site: www.westernhorseman.com.